Kathleen —

A world traveller and talent. Keep your spirit and enthusiasm curiosity.

5/2002

Jessica Stockwell's

DARE to Travel the World
A Mini Manifesto for Globetrotters

Jessica Stockwell

...and may the adventures continue --.

Jim

St. Barthélemy Press
Atlanta, Georgia 30341
www.saintbartsbooks.com

Printed in the United States of America

ISBN: 1-887617-09-4

Updated Edition
October 12, 2001

This book is dedicated to:
Dollie Allgood
Anita Stockwell
Marguerite Stockwell Grace
and Mrs. Gamble

Women of great courage and inspiration.

This Updated Edition is dedicated to the ON THE GO
People and Faces (see People & Faces---acknowledgements
page), the travel industry, the travelling public and those who
shared stories and conversations with me along my
journey September 11-26 to capture a sense of
events and their implications.

DARE to Travel the World

Contents

Acknowledgements

Everyone with whom I've had a conversation or of whom I've asked a question in the past 10 years has contributed to my research and helped form my observations about international travel and the traveling public. You've all helped me understand and piece together relationships between intercultural, verbal, nonverbal and technological communications.

Thanks to all of you for being open to spontaneous
conversation; don't let the conversation die.

In the immediate conversation, I want to thank Steve, my soulmate, partner and love of my life; my immediate family, for always being my family and a support system I'm blessed to have: Betty Stockwell Grace and Charles Stockwell; my brothers and sisters, Clinton, Jeffrey, Elizabeth, Charlie and Jacqueline; my half-sister, Ashley and my half-brother, Nathan. I want to thank my lovely nieces, Lily, Ruby, Alley, Anna and Winter Marie and my nephew, Kyle; my extended relations, sisters one and all: Julie Sabo, Laurie Leider, Teresa Lindley, Margie Ehrlichmann, Martha Mars, Ginny Schutz, Selome and Elleni Haileleoul, Elsa Girma, Valerie Smith and Leyla Lazoglu.

This book wouldn't be in print if it weren't for Walt Fuller and St. Barthélemy Press; thank you for your conversation and interest sparked in 1998 and for your patience over time. Thank you, Deborah Butler, Ph.D., a neighbor and friend whose openness and conversation have been a great support along the journey. Rick Thomas, a mischievous collaborator, thank you for listening to rants and raves and comparing notes on publishing, process, trends and techniques in multimedia and the Internet. And Sallie Wallace, thank you for your perspective and meticulous report on Prague. A timely contribution.

Thanks, too, to editorial consultants and advisors, Susan Pilgrim, Ph.D. and Bob Cylinder. To Georgia Dzurica, a writing professional and creative talent, thank you for helping me get this out the door! And to Marcia O'Grey, for having the patience, enthusiasm and energy to handle all the translation sections. Plus a special thanks to Chris Coleman for allowing me to follow her lead in the world of publishing and learn through her experience.

Thanks to Aquilina Mawadza, a lecturing professor from Zimbabwe, who generously translated the Zimbabwe 10 Highly Effective Words to "Get By" section into Shona in response to an email from a complete stranger just days before production. Thank you, Cameron Smith, with the Shona Language Web site, for facilitating this.

Thank you to François Michel, who sent email to help me make some important decisions at the last minute; Milchen de Vasconcelos, Esther Sworney and Mark Ellinger, travel industry insiders and experts who know the global travel, tourism and airline markets and shared their knowledge and insights. And thanks to other globetrotters, including Randy Whiting, Robert Pee, Kathy Thomas, Janis Cannon (another around-the-world champion), Chris McGinnis, Ken Parris and Jim Murphy–all folks practiced and masterful in travelling on short notice.

On the technology and communications side: Thanks to the 1998 board members of WIT, Women in Technology, Atlanta–a community of women providing a voice for the talent, skills and communications of girls and women in today's world. Thanks for fostering awareness and recognition for women in the technology fields. Thank you, Bob Wachtel, for helping me launch a Web-based email service in 1997 and keeping the endless possibilities of Internet communications alive. A personal thanks to Julie Jacobs and Carl Selinger, pioneers in technology and adventure.

And a universal thanks to the community of cybercafes, trailblazing public Internet service providers and airports along the way. Now I know I can work and play anywhere on the planet!

People & Faces

ATLANTA

New York

Washington, D.C.

September 5-26, 2001

DARE to Travel the World

Introduction

Think of this book as a call to move forward, or better yet, a heart-pumping, soul-stirring yell to move outside your comfort zone and your complacency. You'll need patience and all your skills in adapting to unfamiliar and uncertain circumstances. You and I are challenged to get on with our lives with the understanding that we have little control over those circumstances.

We aren't going to stop travelling. Whether locally, nationally or internationally, travel will continue. This book reveals a new approach to travel that offers globetrotters adaptive techniques. As you plan your trip, organizing your information, testing your aptitudes and adjusting your expectations are key to adapting. This call to move forward will challenge your comfort level and beg courage to regain confidence in the travel industry, which is committed to making your travel experience a good and safe one.

At the heart of this book is my 1996 around-the-world trip. In an attempt to share that adventure, I've packaged each of my destinations into an easy-to-read-and-absorb format—12 chapters, or what I call "heads-up" destination profiles. The HOW IT WORKS page follows.

This book speaks to the traveller who has the courage to move forward in unfamiliar situations and surroundings. Page through this collection of information, vivid images and recollections of tastes, sounds and smells that will give you a preview of places you've read about—places you may be going to yourself in the near future.

Globetrotters are masterful at developing a "lightness of being," or adaptability. Many own an inherent understanding of humanity and the openness to discover the beauty that exists everywhere. DARE to continue your journey, near or far, to meet the people of the world. One thing you'll discover is that you can find many of them right in your own neighborhood, office or school.

Today, road warriors are passé. You and I are the travellers of today. I DARE myself to move forward and continue my journey, with no end in site. I encourage you to do the same. In fact, I DARE you!

Why a Mini Manifesto for Globetrotters and How it Works

Travelling to new and unfamiliar places, living out of carry-on luggage and sleeping in a different bed every 2 to 3 days for 6 months led to UNLEARNING and letting go of many habits, ideas and beliefs. On my trip, rituals of the usual were dashed and challenged along the way. So new tactics were developed to handle one day at a time. Face the unfamiliar with courage and view reality with compassion. And keep movin' forward, upmarket, down-market and in between.

How it Works

Thinking about a destination? In one or two words, mentally, answer these 5 questions:

1. WHY   Why are you travelling? Vacation? Business?
A little bit of both?

2. WHO   Who is travelling? You, your colleagues,
family, friends, pets?

3. WHAT   What kind of traveller are you? Self-directed?
Used to creature comforts? Well- travelled?
A new traveller? A special-needs traveller?
A whiny traveller? A free sprit?

4. WHEN   At what time of year are you planning to travel?
Is it your choice or an obligation?

5. WHERE   Where are you going?

Just thinking about the answers to these questions jumpstarts a process of assessment and evaluation that I categorize into 3 checks or tactics.

Each 6-page chapter includes a **Worldly-wise Travel Perspectives** section. Vivid images, striking observations, tastes and smells that invoke memories, discoveries and magical moments. The 3 checks: a **Reality Check**, **Cultural Check** and a **Communications Check**. The Reality, Cultural and Communications Checks, along with the Comfort Zone Challenges sections, are techniques to organize information to heighten your awareness as you adjust to unfamiliar or new situations. Each section includes a side fact or recommendation and a 'heads-up' rating: Great, Good, A Challenge, Dodgy and Caution. Take 3 mental checks before you go anywhere, Chattanooga or China. Thinking of your destination in these terms will help you prepare to move outside your comfort zone and adapt to the circumstances at hand. And I couldn't complete this without including the **Comfort Zone Challenges** section and a politely put toilet story or two. Enjoy, pass it along, use it.

Basic Stuff

■ Get a passport. Go to your local passport office or travel.state.gov online and get the paperwork done. You never know, you may be ready to travel the world on short notice.

Take a REALITY CHECK

Balance destination realities, which are facts and current situations particular to a locale, with your expectations. Your expectations are gathered from the glossy magazines, brochures and travel guides showing happy people everywhere. It's always sunny. And you expect to make your way around just as you do back home, though Istanbul, the city you are contemplating visiting is a compact, urban, modern metropolis with a population of 9 million.

Once you quickly scan the 10 destination realities, you will realize that Istanbul is huge and congested. Some people in the hospitality industry speak English, but language can be an obstacle. The country is politically volatile and economically struggling. Istanbul has a new millennium-ready airport; allow 3 hours to get there from the city center and 1.5 hours for check in. These are some facts and information to express the destination's reality. Now, use this information to visualize a picture of what you will actually encounter once you arrive. That's a Reality Check.

Take a CULTURAL CHECK

Develop a culturally conscious attitude and carry it with you wherever you go. Spend more time listening, so that you observe and respond in an appropriate manner to make a good first impression. Dress appropriately, not too loud or too casually, depending on the circumstances. Try to read other people for visual cues.

Leave your ego behind so that you are keenly aware of your surroundings. Ask questions and show interest. Make an effort to fit in, but be yourself; you shouldn't adjust your behavior to the immediate circumstances. Experience the destination fully. That's a Cultural Check.

Take a COMMUNICATIONS CHECK

Take note of the 10 Highly Effective Words to "GET BY." This is a requirement for today's traveller. This page is designed to be torn out and taken with you. Use it at every opportunity when interacting with local people. They will appreciate the effort, and you'll probably learn more quickly. That's a Communications Check.

This page is now revised with airport and airline updates. The back side is a map of my around-the-world trip taken in 1996. Use the blank section for jotting down addresses, phone numbers, notes on people and places you meet, passwords and anything you want. Fold it up and keep it with you for reference.

> **GREAT**
> **GOOD**
> **A CHALLENGE**
> **DODGY**
> **CAUTION**

What the Ratings Mean

These descriptive words reflect how I, as a North American traveller, view a country's 10 "Destination Realities."

GREAT—Means I was able to adapt easily no matter what the circumstances were---expected or unexpected---to have a wonderful experience.

GOOD—Means I was able to adjust expectations and behavior to the circumstances in order to have the best possible experience.

A CHALLENGE—Means the environment in the host country is so different that it challenges Western and North American sensibilities, standards and behavior.

DODGY—A polite way to say that I was more than a bit repulsed by a situation or circumstances. Conditions needed attention or improvement.

CAUTION—Means that you need to be aware of customs, social norms and/or the local government. You may inadvertently do something that is misinterpreted. You may be in danger because of the local circumstances, or because your Western affluence attracts people who will try to take advantage of you.

■ Look for a rating with each **Destination Reality** and **Comfort Zone** section for a quick heads-up.

Our deepest fear is not that we are
inadequate.
Our deepest fear is that we are powerful
beyond measure.
It is our light, not our darkness,
that most frightens us.
We ask ourselves,
who am I to be brilliant,
gorgeous, talented and fabulous?

You are a child of God.
Your playing small
doesn't serve the world.
There's nothing enlightened about shrinking
so that other people won't feel insecure
around you.
We were born to make manifest
the glory of God that is within us;
it's in everyone.

And as we let our own light shine,
we unconsciously give other people permission
to do the same.
As we are liberated from our own fear,
our presence automatically liberates others.

- Nelson Mandela

Russia

Russia

St. Petersburg & Environs

St. Petersburg---Catherine the Great splashed the city with Baroque and Rococo and did a fabulous job at that. Queen Catherine took interior design to the outer limits---the city was her interior and the influence of Renaissance Europe her designer. Grand scale pastel exteriors, bejeweled and ornate stone interiors, intrigue and charming canalled streets mix to offer grandeur of the past. Ballet and mass transit.

DISCOVERIES

■ *The St. Petersburg Times, online and offline.*
■ *Vodka was cheaper than water.*
■ *We could survive in a hostel with a set of 5 single beds, a common bathroom for 8 and NO hot water for 6 days.*
■ *Internet access was available through a computer in the common room with a Netscape browser. Sent Email from Boris and Natasha...new mischievous destination identities created while in Russia.*
■ *The underground subway is as grand as you hear. Felt safe in the hordes of moving St. Petersburgers.*

■ *Interpreting directions and maps in Cyrillic is an interesting challenge and one that tests patience, pattern recognition and nonverbal communications (lots of pointing and head shaking). Making it through the maze of subways and streets by map on any level offers rewards with wonderful successes and new discoveries.*
■ *Signage is limited and generally in Cyrillic so checking a guidebook or local English newspaper is a great help. Tapping into the English speaking expatriate community is always an option.*

MAGICAL MOMENTS

■ *June - "White Nights." 24 hours of daylight was a strange but delightful motivation to keep going in a charming city waking up to Spring.*
■ *Ad hoc tickets were procured, sinisterly but legally, outside the Mariinski Theatre just minutes before a premiere performance of Don Quixote. The theatre, the performance and people were a wonderful mix of pride*

and worldliness.
■ *Stopping in an Irish pub (where I imagined the Irish Mafia hangs out hobnobbing with expatriates) was a subculture slice of life. Enjoyed chips, a beer and recounted the last 24 hours with no nightfall. We were awake many, many hours in transit.*
■ *Running 2 miles from the theatre area to our hostel in broad daylight to make the midnight curfew when the doors are locked.*

Destination Realities

"Best Practice" Travel Advice

POPULATION
4.5 million plus
`GOOD`

Check the Tourist Office in the city or pay for a guided tour to gain a quick overview of the city. Use guidebooks and translations to communicate with public services and restaurants. Manageable-sized city---easy to get around with maps. You gain a sense of familiarity in 1 to 3 days. An effort to attract young Russian professionals has been successful, which balances and flavors the population. There's a mix of dilapidated and renovated buildings contrasting new and old, reflecting a changing population.

WEATHER
4 seasons, avoid winter
`GOOD`

Avoid winter unless you're on business and/or taken care of by friends or business associates. The Russian Federation is a massive country geographically, with diverse weather patterns. Spring, summer or fall are optimal times to visit. Summer can be sticky with extremes and no A/C is the general status except in upmarket establishments. June is known as "White Nights." 24 hours of daylight occurs sometime during the month of June. Solstice---long daylight hours allow you to get much accomplished, weather permitting. June is good.

TRANSPORT
1st walk, 2nd hire car
`GOOD`

Airport - Aeroport
Train - Poezd
Bus - autoboos
Subway - metro
Taxi - Taksi
Where is - gde

Walking is the best practice. The subway is one of the best and most conventional modes of transportation. A hired car is recommended for business travel---done through a reputable service or concierge. Local buses are too much of a challenge unless you're escorted or coached along the way. Language and signage in Cyrillic limits ease of visit for short-term visitors. Walking is a delightful preference through canalled streets and an 18th-century city center.

PEDESTRIAN-FRIENDLY
9 on a scale of 1-10
`GREAT`

Walking is great. Always use caution at night. This historical city center is based on a pedestrian community. Walking through the city is engaging. Sidewalks lined with canals, bridges and passageways of times past are the root of a pedestrian-centered lifestyle that is refreshing. This is a great city to get around in and see...for business, pleasure and adventure.

MONEY
RUBLES (RUB)
`DODGY`

A cash economy. Credit cards are accepted for payment only in a few high-priced hotels, restaurants and stores. Traveler checks are not widely accepted. U.S. dollars (hard currency) are desirable but must be exchanged. Avoid shady and too-good-to-be-true exchanges. ATMs (Bancomat) are available and exchange stands are plentiful. Better exchange is in city with small percentage variations. For large sums, ask 5-star hotel for best recommendation. Beware of passing tattered bills; most places tend to only accept new, crisp $100.00 bills.

| GREAT |
| GOOD |
| A CHALLENGE |
| DODGY |
| CAUTION |

POLLUTION REALITY
8 on a scale of 1-10
GOOD

Be prepared for some days of moderately heavy pollution, especially in the summer. Because of a high percentage of pedestrian traffic, St. Petersburg has been spared the crushing pollution many large cosmopolitan cities experience with 21st-century automobiles and industry. St. Petersburg has moved into a more balanced economy, including more importation of consumer products and services, limiting heavy manufacturing and refineries to the outskirts of the city.

LANGUAGE
Russian, Cyrillic written
A CHALLENGE

Limited English is spoken by many tourism professionals and not spoken by the general public. To ease communications and time constraints, English-speaking guides, tours and guidebooks are recommended. Also a pad and paper can help when communicating. Marketing and signage when available are in Cyrillic. Follow maps and bone up on recognizing phonetic spellings of words and places. Use nonverbal communications like pointing to maps or pre-scripted Cyrillic. Check local language tips from resources and guidebooks. .

POLITICAL REALITY
Russian Federation
A CHALLENGE

Capital: Moscow

Multiparty Federal Republic (10-15 parties). Politics unstable. Check online or offline with State Department warnings to be cognizant of general status for travelling Westerners. Avoid demonstrations. Politics and business go hand in hand. Best practice is to keep opinions to yourself, but show interest in topics and be familiar with politicians names. Consensus is not in the dialogue. Negotiations are long and dramatic. Choose patience.

ECONOMIC REALITY
5 on a scale of 1-10
CAUTION

For visitors: You are generally welcome. People are generally helpful to visitors if they can be. Tourism and international business bring money into the economy. Consumer goods and imports are in high demand by a growing-ever-so-slowly, middle class. Don't flash cash or give the apperance of money. They know you have it if you're there. The majority are in a poor economic state and live in extremely bleak conditions. Many like to learn from Westerners. Others take advantage. Be careful.

AIRPORT FACILITIES
Airport Code: LED
City Code: LED
GOOD

Other Airports:
Moscow - Largest/Main
Kiev and many others

☛ URBAN CTR
7-10 miles
30-40 minutes
$5-20USD

☛ ✈ ALLOW
2 hrs. for check-in
3 hrs. transport

Pulkovo International Airport, St. Petersburg. Secondary airport compared to Russia's main airport in Moscow. Pulkovo 2 new International terminal. English and Cyrillic signage helps facilitate directions. Limited amenities. Be leery of taxis or cabs. Try to arrange pick-up/delivery in advance through reliable contacts. Public bus available to center. Visit **www.pulkovo.ru/english** *for available information.*

BE POLITE: *Listen and observe.*

HAVE MANNERS: *Dress and behave as others around you.*

SHOW INTEREST: *Leave your ego behind, ask questions diplomatically.*

MAKE AN EFFORT: *Fit in. Interact. Engage.*

BE POLITE

Listen and observe learned tendencies of keeping to one's own business. Note people's busy schedules. Don't be loud in public. Waiting is a key characteristic that sometimes teeters on an appearance of apathy or non-interest. A handshake is a common greeting gesture. Kisses on the cheek are reserved for good friends, in personal and professional settings.

HAVE MANNERS

Observe, accept and/or mimic mannerisms. Dress to city code, not flashy or attention-getting, not too colorful. Forget the jewelry. Keep gestures to a minimum. No slaps on the back until someone familiar to you does it to you first, otherwise observe reserved nature. Check loud language and loud laughing at the border.

SHOW INTEREST

General---be open to people's help, but be cautious of uninvited offers for help. Food is expensive. A majority of fruits and vegetables are imported. A major staple is starchy, tasty casseroles and stew-like dishes. Try the specialties and local foods. Vodka is cheap. Be careful when drinking so you won't be taken advantage of in unfamiliar surroundings. Some vodka and liquor are bootleg and dangerous. Use caution. Topics---pick up a local English newspaper and see what's in the news. Show interest in local social concerns, common interests of family and everyday life.

MAKE AN EFFORT

Try local restaurants and local suggestions. Learn what you have in common with people you're interacting with. Try to use a few words of the language and use subtle gestures. Your first impressions either stake you as an "affluent Westerner" or traveller. Paying attention to your behavior and mannerisms will benefit you in business or leisure. Find expat hangouts to ease into local social circles and life.

10 Highly Effective Words to "Get By"

1. A Greeting	zDRA SVTZ ya	zdravsteuyte
2. Please	pa-JALWIS-ta	pazhaluysta
3. Thank You	s-pa SEE ba	spasibo
4. Yes	dah	da
5. No	nYEt	net
6. Toilet	TOO lyet	tualet
7. How Much	s KAW ly ka	skolko
8. Help	pa MAW chi	pomoci
9. Excuse Me	eez vi NI tzya	izvinite
10. Police	mi LEE tzya	militzya

Great Connections & Community

Jot down important phone numbers, contacts, addresses. Great shops and restaurants---get their Email and Web Address.
SCRIBBLE NOTES and info before, during and after!

Airport & Airline Update

St. Petersburg Int'l Airport **www.pulkovo.ru/english**
Relatively new site with general information on terminals. No current check-in or passenger advisory posted. General information posted.

Aeroflot Airlines **www.aeroflot.com**
Review of flights and general list of airline safety directives. No current advisories, but there should be some forthcoming. Contacts available.

RNTO-Russian National Tourist Office
www.russia-travel.com
Good general resource. Direct contact via email recommended for specific questions. Good general heads-up travel tips.

Moving Forward Advisory: Budget 2 hours check-in time at the airport prior to scheduled departure for domestic flights and 3 hours for International flights. Check with your air carrier. Extra security procedures will affect departures.

TEAR out & TAKE

15

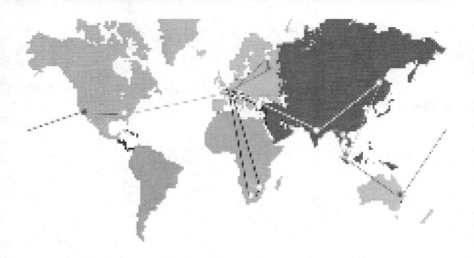

> GREAT
> GOOD
> A CHALLENGE
> DODGY
> CAUTION

Personal Space
A CHALLENGE

Toilets
DODGY

Cleanliness & Bugs
GOOD

PEOPLE SPACE & PERSPIRATION

Personal space: A challenge. Depending on where you come from, a city of 4.5+ million is rather crowded. Subways and streets keep very busy. Life is expensive so living quarters and hotel and/or hostel space is tight. Expect small rooms and limited public space. People are used to living with the bare essentials, shared facilities and maintaining close proximity to each other. Yours and your neighbors' hygiene become apparent. Tolerance instead of complaining is best practice.

TOILETS & TRIBULATIONS

Toilets: A challenge. Always carry a few swatches of toilet paper. Most facilities are Western style. A toilet many times consists of a separate closet or room with flush or pull cord. Sink and tub are generally in a separate room. Public toilets are available but not as plentiful as you may be used to. Public toilets are usually maintained by women attendees who expect tips---these are their wages. Don't expect wash towels and service. Standards vary. Be happy toilets are rather available.

HYGIENE & HIGH JINKS

Drink bottled water. Best practice is to brush teeth with bottled water and wash face separately with bottled water. Keep water out of eyes. Keep food out of sleeping accommodations or you and those that had food before you invite bugs. The more Western and expensive the hotel, the more they are attentive to Western guests. General clean standards apply.

BUGS:

Crawling bugs exist as in most cities. Seasonal mosquitoes enter through windows with no screens.

Western Style

and everything
inbetween

Asian Style

Toilet Stories...

ST. PETERSBURG

Mid-range accommodations have been limited to a few international hostels to house international visitors. Community-type accommodations had a group of up to 8 people sharing a "bath"---a room with a tub, shower hose and sink and a separate toilet closet, which was cleaned daily. Unique toilet rituals came about when in springtime, no heat and still chilly, the hot water disappeared for about a week. Every day I hosed myself with cold, icy water from the hand-held shower hose. At least I could strategically aim and rinse at quick staccato-like intervals with the hose. I washed my hair every other day in the third-floor kitchen sink before anyone got up. I heated water in a pan and then rinsed my hair with warm water in the kitchen sink, a comical trick in itself. I quickly developed a resistance to bathing. I hated to lose body heat going through these rituals. So, I did have clean toilets, but NO hot water. I found out the water is turned off every year in different quadrants of the city. Everyone lives with it, surely I could...and I did.

Switzerland

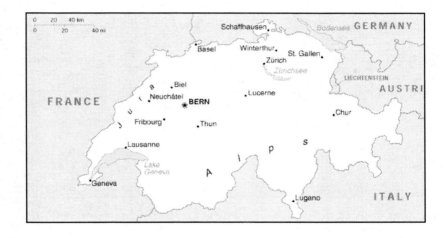

Switzerland
Zurich & Environs

MEMORIES

Picture-perfect landscapes. A tidy city offering top-notch roads to drive independently in stylish compact cars. No highway route numbers but "destination" signs: Zurich, Geneva, Montreux. Making it out of the city of Zurich to the pastoral mountains and lakes, destination: Chatel St. Denis. Comfort, safety and amenities of the affluent Western lifestyle. Full-bodied wine, sumptuous cheese and fresh breads.

DISCOVERIES

■ Mexican food, any food for that matter, costs a lot of money. In Vevey, home of natural waters bottled to drink worldwide, a Margarita cost $10.50 U.S. Ouch!

■ Western wealth and affluence revealed itself with delightful shops full of linens, housewares, trinkets and...romantic eating establishments.

■ A stroll along the lake of Geneva is soothing and visually inviting. It is real.

■ A cybercafe in the Zurich Hauptbahnhof (train station) and the ADAM in Montreux allowed communications in the manner to which I am accustomed---electronically.

■ Buses work on the honor system. Understanding the ticketing and punching ritual is a challenge unless explained in English.

■ Buses and trains run on time---Swiss time---so don't be late. Swatch---the world watchmaker, invented "Internet Time." Watch for it in the future as a measure of time in the new economy.

■ Cows graze and their bells ring, lovely dings and dongs.

MAGICAL MOMENTS

■ Walking from the chalet, about 1.5 miles, to the Chatel St. Denis town center was fairy-tale like through the woods and over the river. Local patisseries, markets and bakeries fill the senses and taunt the appetite.

■ Driving in the dark to the chalet and finding the key hidden under the right rock, placed there 4 months earlier, was a successful adventure. Entering a comfortable, safe haven was indeed soothing. Thank you, **Milchen and Carlos**.

■ Feeling cool blades of grass under my feet while inhaling a view of snowcapped mountains and limitlessness.

Destination Realities   "Best Practice" Travel Advice

POPULATION
1 million
`GREAT`

Check the Tourist Office or hotel concierges for advice and recommendations. Airlines are good sources also. Zurich is considered the heart of Europe in many people's eyes. The population is somewhat homogeneous in appearance, but diverse in history and cultural makeup. The city bustles, showcasing European trends, glitzy wealth and a new generation inviting change. The country is 7 million in population and it takes 3 hours to drive across. A tidy, easy city to get to know in 1 to 2 days. World class and worldly.

WEATHER
4 seasons, any season
`GOOD`

Switzerland is one of the most geographically diverse countries in a condensed area. All seasons offer year-round living and sport. Zurich is a bit overcast and rainy too many days out of the year to give it a stellar rating, but anytime is a great time to visit. Not too many extremes. Be prepared for no air conditioning in many resort areas, midrange hotels or rental cars. You can always get warm or find shelter in rain or snow. Transportation moves through any weather to get you from A to B.

TRANSPORT
1st walk, 2nd bus/taxi
`GREAT`

Airport - der flughafen
Train - die Bahn
Bus - der Bus
Subway - die U-Bahn
Taxi - das Taxi
Where is - Wo ist

Zurich is a central hub for rail and air transport in Europe. The recently renovated rail station, Hauptbahnhof, has an underground mecca of shops and point-of-transit amenities accessible 24-hours-a-day. A cybercafe/restaurant in the main terminal is great. Public transport---the train from airport to city center, buses and trams, work like clockwork offering excellent transport options. Taxis are expensive and securing tickets from the kiosks for buses is tricky. Check English-speaking assistance resources for best approach.

PEDESTRIAN-FRIENDLY
9 on a scale of 1-10
`GREAT`

Compact, cobblestoned and divided into old and new by a river streaming its way to the lake make the city ultra quaint. Walk around to discover the trendy and traditional sections. Trams and buses are readily available to hop on and off. Maps are available. A map helps you and others should you get lost or need assistance. Although Zurich is visitor-friendly, the choice of renting cars bring very strict car-parking rules. Public parking is limited and city street parking is difficult to find. Opt for public transport.

MONEY
SWISS FRANC (SFR)
`GOOD`

Switzerland is famous as a repository for monies from all over the world. Money exchange is available in the many places you would expect, like ATMs and banks. Switzerland has one of the highest costs of living. Switzerland is not a participating EU (European Union) member. Currency issues affecting goods and services work independently from other EU participating countries. Most visits are very expensive. Package deals and preplanning offer the best value for money.

GREAT
GOOD
A CHALLENGE
DODGY
CAUTION

Destination Realities   "Best Practice" Travel Advice   CAUTION

POLLUTION REALITY
8 on a scale of 1-10
GOOD

Pollution invades growing cities. Zurich gets high marks on the pollution scale, but it does have some local industries close to the city center that contribute to the challenge of environmental control. Switzerland is a leader on environmental policy, which is admired worldwide. This commitment has helped to preserve the cities, their rural and resort areas. Watch your trash habits. Take responsibility for anything you discard. There is probably a law on the books for the "proper" way to dispose of it. Ask if unsure.

LANGUAGE
Swiss German, French
A CHALLENGE

Switzerland, uniquely, holds four languages as "official" languages: German, French, Italian and Romansch. Travel and commerce professionals usually have a good command of English. German and French butt heads as dominating languages. Those who expect English to be the prevailing language will be surprised. English is not spoken by everyone, but many signs and most information in print can be found in English as well as five to six other languages.

POLITICAL REALITY
Swiss Confederation
GOOD

Capital: Bern

Ethnocentric values from German, Italian, French and Romansch make up the Swiss population and drive a proud Swiss nationalism. At the same time diverse regional issues and not joining in direct membership in the EU (European Union) have created heated debates and discord. 28 Cantons (counties) make up the constituency of the Swiss Confederation.

ECONOMIC REALITY
8 on a scale of 1-10
GOOD

A unifying EU force on the continent has affected Switzerland. Switzerland is not a direct member of the EU. Pressure on traditions, like the military requirements, the banking industry and environmental issues, are continually on center stage. With practically no unemployment the younger generation is working in and around the powers that be to encourage change. Tourism and the hospitality industries are strong economic forces that continue to keep Switzerland growing.

AIRPORT FACILITIES
Airport Code: ZRH
City Code: ZRH
GREAT

Other Airports:
Geneva
Bern

☛ URBAN CTR
8 miles
20 - 40 minutes
$6 - 25. USD

☛ ✈ ALLOW
1.5 hrs. check-in
1 hr. transport

*Kloten International Airport, Zurich, is one of the greatest airports...in my humble opinion. Two grocery stores chock-full of take-away fresh foods, goodies and cheese. A chocolate manufacturer is on premise. Meeting rooms, lounges, and day rooms for those who need a quick nap, and showers are available. FREE luggage carts go anywhere, even up and down the escalators. Check **www.zurich-airport.ch**.*

BE POLITE: *Listen and observe.*

HAVE MANNERS: *Dress and behave as others around you.*

SHOW INTEREST: *Leave your ego behind, ask questions diplomatically.*

MAKE AN EFFORT: *Fit in. Interact. Engage.*

BE POLITE

The general Swiss population is comfortable with tradition and rituals of respect in the most appropriate manner. Proper etiquette and protocol is expected in all interactions. Each region takes on a flavor of the cultural heritage it holds. A handshake is a common greeting in formal and general informal introductions. An embrace or a kiss on the cheek, for the familiar, varies by region. A more casual business or professional style of interaction is growing in Switzerland and across Europe. The new generation of globetrotting professionals is influencing more open and real-time communications.

HAVE MANNERS

As a neutral country, Switzerland has a reputation for hospitality and caters to visitors. Interestingly, the general population is watchful of outsiders. You are expected to be knowledgeable about the rules and laws the locals adhere to. Inquire with a confidante or resource for proper etiquette in uncertain situations.

SHOW INTEREST

The traditional Swiss culture is celebrated nationally, while there are distinct German, Italian and French subcultures coexisting. There is a delightful flavor of many traditions of bordering countries. Different value systems exist and topics of discussion should be adapted and respectful to your locale. The Swiss are a proud and tolerant society as a whole, but 21st-century influences and issues reveal a very protective and slow-to-change faction and social climate.

MAKE AN EFFORT

It's easy to absorb and engage in the natural beauty, rich prosperity and historical treasures the Swiss offer to visitors. A common appreciation of nature and the culture make engaging conversation. Don't let a socially more reserved and conservative population cloud the discoveries of a new generation preserving, yet changing, Switzerland in the 21st century.

10 Highly Effective Words to "Get By"

1. A Greeting	GOO-ten-TUHG	Gutten Tag
2. Please	Bee-tuh	bitte
3. Thank You	DHUN-kuh	danke
4. Yes	y-AH	ja
5. No	nein	nein
6. Toilet	das vie-TSEE, die toy-LEH-tuh	das WC, die toilette
7. How Much	vi-Fil KAWS-tet das	vievel kostet das
8. Help	HEHL-fen	helfen
9. Excuse Me	aynt-SHOOL-dea-gen zee	entschuldigen Sie
10. Police	paw-leet-ZAY	der polizei

Great Connections & Community

Jot down important phone numbers, contacts, addresses. Great shops and restaurants---get their Email and Web Address.
SCRIBBLE NOTES and info before, during and after!

Airport & Airline Update

Zurich Int'l Airport   **www.uniqueairport.com**
Newly designed, site managed by outside sources. Contemporary with informational content and contacts for Airport questions.

Swissair   **www.swissair.com**
A comprehensive site with daily postings, update advisories and media announcements regarding airline status. This airline is resuming flight schedules gradually; check here for changes and adjustments in US scheduled flights. Site has time-sensitive updates, news briefs and contact info.

Switzerland Tourism   **www.switzerlandtourism.com**
A comprehensive and updated site. Excellent reference and info.

Moving Forward Advisory: Budget 1.5 hours check-in time at the airport prior to scheduled departure for domestic flights and 2 hours for International flights. Check with your air carrier 72 hours in advance. Extra security measures are in place.

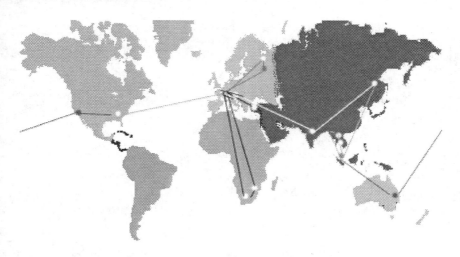

> GREAT
> GOOD
> A CHALLENGE
> DODGY
> CAUTION

Personal Space
GOOD

Toilets
GREAT

Cleanliness & Bugs
GREAT

PEOPLE SPACE & PERSPIRATION

Owning property is very expensive so real estate and housing are at a premium. Personal space is provided in open, natural surroundings more than in spacious rooms, apartments and housing. General mannerisms are conservative and one keeps to his or her own space and distance, not a lot of in-your-face contact. So unless you are very "sportif" you and those around you won't be perspiring a lot. Invading one's personal space is an impolite intrusion.

TOILETS & TRIBULATIONS

Very clean usually. In many homes and business establishments the toilet and bath are separate. Many use a bidet. Pay toilets exist and are a popular practice in some public venues. Western standards apply and there are plenty of toilets to serve the toilet-going public.

HYGIENE & HIGH JINKS

Tidy and controlled. Every city has accommodations that are a bit cheesy. But Switzerland has high standards and a reputation to uphold. The good news is they usually do. More time to put energies into eating, drinking and taking in the sites.

BUGS:

Not many to worry about. You'll find them in nature. Be aware of any advisories in rural and mountain areas.

Western Style

and everything
i n b e t w e e n

Asian Style

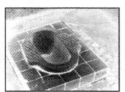

Toilet Stories...

SWITZERLAND

I rebel against pay toilets. Switzerland reminds me of pay toilets and a pay-toilet-traumatic-moment I'll always remember.

Eating and drinking cautiously is a strategy usually reserved for destinations like India, when you travel for 5-6 hours at a stretch never knowing when the next toilet stop will be. Here in Switzerland, no worries. It's clean, tidy, civilized one might say, and Western-amenity rich. During a 3-hour drive from Montreux to Zurich I urgently had to go, so I jumped out of the car at a road/gastation stop. A busload of tourists pulled up at the same time. I rushed to the ladies room, wanting desperately to beat the onslaught of German and Swiss ladies heading the same way. I elbowed my way through, only to be completely incensed and pushed out of line because I didn't have the correct change to get into the PAY toilet. These matrons were condescending, avoiding eye contact and ignoring, collectively, my pleas in German for change. They made sure the toilet door closed after them. No mercy! I was outraged to have to pay to pee. I contemplated relieving myself on the floor...I didn't. I found change. I curse pay toilets to this day and will rebel the next time I am confronted with one. Bet they don't charge for using a stall in the men's room. FREE PAY TOILETS!

South Africa

South Africa
Cape Town & Environs

MEMORIES

Vivid textures of land and water. The Cape of Good Hope offers physical colliding of 2 oceans and many peoples. South Africa struggles with a new and challenged government. Learned fears and everything in between flavor everyday life. A new sense of pride is revealed through peoples' smiles and approach. African music, myth and spirit draw you in to explore with confidence. Meat pies, South African wine and curry soup.

DISCOVERIES

■ *Cape Town now includes townships and it's a redrawn city.*
■ *Wired: went down to the I@Cafe during a cold rainy day to catch up on life in general, checked in back home, and met new friends. A woman next to me was crying and chatting online to distant friends for hours.*
■ *Cape Town has many issues to address as a new world-class city.*
■ *Champagne - South African champagne--tasty and delightful.*
⊟*Flora and fauna, sea creatures and tasty curry squash soup.*

■ *Xhosa peoples and the Transkei---life in another style and time. Fear not unless you come bejeweled, toting Western amenities resembling a sparkling candy in a desert rather than an intruding-ever-so-delicately curious traveller.*
■ *Africa Time means different things to different groups. Time loses strictness bending to consideration of means. Trains can run a couple of hours late---give into Africa time with understanding.*
■ *Wine country, townships and cybercafes.*

MAGICAL MOMENTS

■ *Wild, crisp winds. Walking the paths and stretches of lands along the expansive Cape Point and environs. Ocean breezes.*
⊟*Sharing discussions with Lee, owner of The Backpack in Cape Town, about the Olympic bid for hosting the 2004 Olympics. Met a local government representative to hear the many issues pro and con.*

■ *Conversations and an introduction to wandering world travellers. Tales of India, Africa, bugs, toilets, groping and the unbelievable beauty in the people and places.*
■ *Opting to trust complete strangers and meeting **Malcolm**, a 'mate' from Perth, Australia. A great travelling friend who added to the perspective and dreams.*

Destination Realities   "Best Practice" Travel Advice

POPULATION
1.5 - 2.5 million
GREAT

Check with local Tourist Office. South Africa is doing a great job of supplying the information you need from a broad perspective. There are many cultural groups with 11 national languages. Carrying preconceived notions inhibits quickly adjusting to social situations. Generally, Western influences are well established in the urban areas with flavors of diverse African groups. All together, albeit with signs of segregation and distinct income levels, the population reflects new thoughts and cooperation. A professional's high-growth city.

WEATHER
hot summers, cool winters
GOOD

Cape Town is south of the Equator. So, if you're coming from the North be aware that the seasons are opposite of what you'd expect. Cape Town sports a breeze that moves diverse weather from other areas around on a daily basis. The Drakensberg Mountain range rises in the East along the coast, just inland, and the Indian and Atlantic oceans meet at Cape Point. Fog is the biggest interruption for visitors trying to capture a view. A beautiful coastal city to visit any time of year. Summer is the most popular visiting season---December to May.

TRANSPORT
1st walk, 2nd car/coach
GREAT

Afrikaans:
Airport - lughwave
Train - trein
Bus - bus
Subway - moltrein
Taxi - taxi
Where is - waar is

The city center is small enough to get around by foot, but there are different areas of Cape Town and environs. For short visits, don't hire (or take) a car. Taking a taxi, shuttle coach or half-day tour is recommended to satisfy the desire to taste more of the diverse landscape of the city and outskirts. Car rentals are comparable with urban expectations for variety, price and services. Rail is available to outskirts of town and outer townships and other cities throughout Africa. Overall it's a good transportation infrastructure.

PEDESTRIAN-FRIENDLY
8 on a scale of 1-10
GOOD

Good for city walking, especially on the waterfront, with specialty shops, unique markets and South African souvenirs and treasures. The city center is commercial and markets are set up and taken down in different areas. Check local times for markets. Nearby country walking is enjoyed by many, along the many beaches, nature reserves and trails on the Cape of Good Hope. Check with a concierge and travel resources for recommended areas and times to be careful of. Be cautious of best times to walk about.

MONEY
South African RAND (ZAR)
GOOD

Exchange varies, but generally the RAND is not as strong against foreign currencies. So goods appear to be generally less expensive. Banking is a big industry throughout South Africa along with strong mining and mineral resources. ATMs are available in major commercial areas, but not plentiful elsewhere. Keep receipts. Carry small amounts of cash for daily purchases, eating, and buying tickets unless in an upmarket area where credit is accepted. Exchange is very favorable for services and products.

GREAT
GOOD
A CHALLENGE
DODGY
CAUTION

Destination Realities   "Best Practice" Travel Advice

POLLUTION REALITY
8 on a scale of 1-10
GOOD

Generally an unpolluted environment due to open lands, flora and fauna, oceans and environmental appreciation and attention. Heavy industry, including mining and fabrication, is located on the outskirts of the city center. The diverse geographical layout of Cape Point and Table Mountain areas fosters breezes, short-term weather patterns and interruptions of rain that refresh the city air.

LANGUAGE
11 official languages
GOOD

Afrikaans, English, Zulu and Xhosa are the most widely spoken official languages. English is widely spoken in urban areas and outside, at times limited to a 'pop' (popular) American English jargon. South African English is a mix of Afrikaans, derived from Dutch with influences of local cultures, groups, diverse English speakers and international television. Get some tips from local contacts and listen carefully to pick up words and local meanings.

POLITICAL REALITY
Multiparty Republic
A CHALLENGE

Capital: Pretoria (administrative)
Cape Town (legislative)
Bloemfontein (judicial)

1991-1994 transitions from a ruling white minority to a black majority has the groups of political alliances split into 6 to 10 parties. A more universal system of governance and government works is being put in place. The three most populous parties are the African National Congress, the National Party and the Zulu Inkatha Party. Cape Town is the legislative center. Pretoria is the Capital and administrative center. Bloemfontein is the judicial center. Politically diverse and changing with challenges.

ECONOMIC REALITY
5 on a scale of 1-10
A CHALLENGE

Belief in apartheid is consistent with past waves of religious influence, recent generations of many in the white minority and a wealthier population. It will take education and generations to change this mindset. Long established fears of past conflict remain in place and are recycled to interfere with economic reform. Local markets and crafts are livelihoods for many adapting to a yet unclear urban life. A healthy dose of optimism is apparent as a new population is empowered. Economic stability on the rise.

AIRPORT FACILITIES
Airport Code: CPT
   City Code: CPT
GOOD

Other Airports:
Johannesburg - Largest
Durban
and many local airports in network

☛ URBAN CTR
24 miles
35 - 60 minutes
$25.00 USD
☛ ✈ ALLOW
1.5 hrs. check-in
2 hrs. transport

Cape Town International Airport, 4 terminals and the 2nd-largest airport facility. Passenger transit is projected for 6 million by 2004. New projects are underway to expand airport and build a common passenger facility to be completed by 2006. Minimum public space, basic facilities and expected amenities. Not a transit hub. New Management. Visit **www.airports.co.za** or contact by telephone the V.I.P. Center (27)(21)937.1233.

BE POLITE: *Listen and observe.*

HAVE MANNERS: *Dress and behave as others around you.*

SHOW INTEREST: *Leave your ego behind, ask questions diplomatically.*

MAKE AN EFFORT: *Fit in. Interact. Engage.*

BE POLITE

Be sensitive to different cultural groups. Religious sensitivity---the Christians constitute the largest group of faiths with major distinctions. Sects include the Afrikaan Reform Church and the Black Independent Churches. Be prepared to respect these differences. Observe different cultural groups and industries and pay attention to their sense of time; an awareness of this is polite. In business settings promptness is expected with leniency. Time and strict adherence to it is often understandably relaxed---it's influenced by the transportation infrastructure and local lifestyles.

HAVE MANNERS

A handshake is a normal greeting gesture. To show respect for all peoples of South Africa is expected. Manners and behavior standards vary depending on the location and group you are interacting with. Many people still harbor resentment from the past towards each other. To get past this be sensitive and observant of all perspectives and treat everyone with equal attention and respect. A more casual dress standard applies across the board.

SHOW INTEREST

Diverse customs and language that have existed independently of each other are now mixing. Standards vary depending on ethnic influence. Be a quick study and adapt to "their" concept of time and lifestyle. Topics of discussion should be general and not investigative about race relations and like topics unless you're invited to express your thoughts. Show interest in topics of sports, technology, industry and music as well as family life.

MAKE AN EFFORT

It's easy to be taken in by the beauty and diversity Cape Town and its environs have to offer. Be open to gestures of interest and offer support for the economy through new tourism efforts. Make an effort to learn something new, gain perspective, take interest in the diverse groups and see beauty through their eyes.

10 Highly Effective Words to "Get By"

Afrikaans

1. A Greeting	ha-LO	hallo
2. Please	AH-se-blief	asseblief
3. Thank You	DAHN-kye	dankie
4. Yes	ee-AH	ja
5. No	NI-eh	nee
6. Toilet	rooss-KOH-mehr	ruskamer
7. How Much	hoe-veel-KOS-dee	hoeviel kos dit
8. Help	HEHL-pern	helpen
9. Excuse Me	vers-KOON my	verskoon my
10. Police	po-LEE-sie	polisie

Great Connections & Community

Jot down important phone numbers/contacts/addresses. Great shops and restaurants---get their Email and Web address. **SCRIBBLE NOTES** and info before, during and after!

Airport & Airline Update

Cape Town Int'l Airport　　　　**www.airports.co.za**
A comprehensive and progressive site covering a network of airports across South Africa. New CEO appointment. Inquire directly by email for current and forthcoming passenger airport security advisories.

South African Airways　　　　**www.flysaa.com**
A comprehensive site with time-sensitive postings covering daily operations and advisories for the public. Content and feature-rich for easy online use and direct bookings. Check site.

South African Tourism
　　　www.southafrica.net/southafricantourism
A contemporary information-rich site. No current travel advisories.

Moving Forward Advisory: Budget 1.5 hours Cape Town, 2 hours Johannesburg for check-in time prior to scheduled departure for domestic flights and 2 hours for International flights. Also, expect traffic and more drive time to get to Johannesburg International airport.

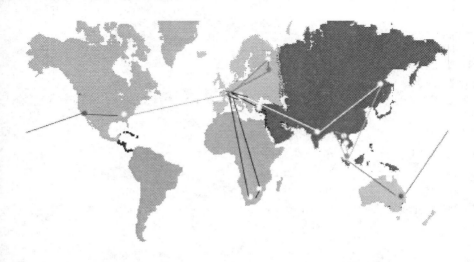

GREAT
GOOD
A CHALLENGE
DODGY
CAUTION

Personal Space
GOOD

Toilets
GOOD

Cleanliness & Bugs
GOOD

PEOPLE SPACE & PERSPIRATION

Cape Town is a hospitable and energetic city. Contentious and non-contentious relations between white and black South Africans reveal themselves in different ways. "No trespassing" signs and barbed wire fences around homes in the city neighborhoods are common. A general separation is recognizable by social class in public areas. Personal space zones are relative to an individual's social and personal background. Respect of personal space should be observed and practiced.

TOILETS & TRIBULATIONS

Cape Town's city center and suburbs offer Western amenities and bathrooms in public establishments. Separate toilets are found in restaurants and some public facilities. They diminish in high standards of cleanliness depending on the grade of the establishment. For example, a corner bakery does not allow use of the toilet even if it serves the public.

Toilets, like many around the world, are not on the "high" priority list in a country needing much. For commercial or private use, standards vary across the board. Rural areas have limited or no public toilets and private toilets offer relief no matter what the condition. Be thankful. Take advantage of going when you can and keep a swatch of toilet paper with you at all times.

HYGIENE & HIGH JINKS

Standards for Western accommodations depend on who runs the place. Check your accommodations to see if it will meet your standards. Opt for limited uncooked food and peelable fruits and vegetables when outside urban areas. A consistent practice is to use bottled water at all times, even when brushing teeth. A world of different microbes exists and can affect individuals in subtle, undetectable ways.

BUGS:

A spacious, open land rich with resources offers minimum bugs and creatures except where you might expect to find them. Urban centers tend to be free of bugs unless in season. Malaria-infected mosquitoes are to be taken seriously in the western and inland parts of South Africa. Also, check suggested shots through a travellers' medical center before departure. Better to be too prepared than suffer the consequences of viruses or sickness. Advised precautions are stated at areas where needed.

Western Style

and everything
inbetween

Asian Style

Toilet Stories...

SOUTH AFRICA

Trains across South Africa were great, albeit a bit shaky. Thus, many taking aim at the Western-style toilets on board missed their intended mark, and train toilets got messy. There are not many public toilet facilities and any available get high usage. Be prepared to go quickly and move on.

Zimbabwe

Zimbabwe
Harare & Environs

A Western colonial bustling city with many hard-working citizens trying to make ends meet. Mama and baby elephants in the bush and crocs in the river. Crazy bungie jumpers leaping from Vic Falls bridge. Views of landscapes and smells of food at stops along the 24-hours turned into 27-hours train ride from Jo'burg to Harare. **Wendy**, *from Canada, an inspiration I met at the accommodations---Overlanders. Chicken on the Braai. Ancient ruins.*

DISCOVERIES

■ *Harare, a modern city in a continuous economic slump.*
■ *A train journey across country is delightful, safe and comfortable. Trains in old style are grand and regal.*
■ *Africa Time---it has different meanings to different groups of people. It depends on the means to get from A to B. Relax and enjoy when you are on Africa Time.*
■ *Colonial town Bulawayo. Turn-of-the-century architecture, lingering grandeur of the past. The National Gallery on Main Street offers insight to life for locals now and past.*

■ *Travellers from everywhere, intent with discovery and learning more across Africa.*
■ *A cybercafe right in the heart of downtown Harare.*
■ *Strong women. Amazing images of women balancing heavy sacks of potatoes, and baskets full of heavy, heavy stuff. One skirt-clad woman balanced one large suitcase in one hand, a larger (60 lbs.) one on her head with her child clinging to her other free hand. Women---an observation of multitasking at its finest in Africa.*
■ *Lessons of animal life on the Hwange game run with our all-knowing guide,* **Watson**.

MAGICAL MOMENTS

■ *Walking through ancient Great Zimbabwe Monument ruins. The sense of History and First "humans."*
■ *Hopping on the train to Victoria Falls with dinner to go: 4 ripe tomatoes, a loaf of bread and a huge avocado for a dime.*
■ *Celebrating the 4th of July under the*

sparkling night skies of Victoria Falls. Memorable sensations of cool mist, warm sun and visions of rainbows in the gorge. A toast to good fortune, fate and destiny.
■ *Farewell to* **Malcolm**, *a travelling companion and friend for life. Cheers mate!*
■ *A spectacular view from the air of Victoria Falls and a herd of elephants.*

Destination Realities   "Best Practice" Travel Advice

POPULATION
1.5 million
GOOD

The city population is 1.5 million. The country population is 11 million and in turmoil at this writing. The first upstanding "humans" populated here more than 4 million years ago. 11th century facades and stone walls are remains of Great Zimbabwe, a former central force and trading capital. The city now holds modern rituals of business and entertainment with colonial, traditional and new technology mixing in to try and stabilize the economy and politics. An easy city to get to know...cautiously.

WEATHER
winter most comfortable
GOOD

May to October prove to be most comfortable and dry with other months hot but dry. A landlocked city and country with a diverse topography. Bushveld and lowlands outside the city. The city is busy in any weather with business and tourism. The city can be grimy due to the dry and dusty environment. Drought is, and has been, a big concern affecting the people, the jobs and their livelihood.

TRANSPORT
1st walk, 2nd taxi
A CHALLENGE

Shona:
Airport - eyapoti
Train - tireni
Bus - bhazi
Taxi - tekisi
Where is - iri kupi

The city is the center of commerce and the country. Local buses, a good train system and a good airline keep people and commerce moving, albeit not strict to scheduled times. Walking about the city is very doable; however, this is not an economically strong time and crime is a problem for locals as well as for international visitors. A recommended taxi service is a preferable way to travel to appointments. Transportation to Victoria Falls and other sites is readily available and reasonable.

PEDESTRIAN-FRIENDLY
6 on a scale of 1-10
A CHALLENGE

A relatively easy downtown to walk in. It grew from a central commerce and trading hub for Southeastern Africa. Pedestrians beware. Two decades of economic strife make times hard for the local urban population. Pockets of unsafe zones are to be expected and avoided by the observant international visitor. While normal best practice is to walk in couples or more during the daytime, extra precaution is suggested at night. Take a taxi or heed the suggestions of your local guide or concierge.

MONEY
ZIM DOLLAR (ZWD)
A CHALLENGE

Zimbabwe inflation has been very high. Those coming from strong-currency countries will find your visit very reasonable. Local goods are available but in short supply. Imported goods are expensive. Artists are a mainstay in the economy and their works are unique and a good value, especially as a means to support themselves. Limited ATMs and upscale establishments take credit cards. Have cash in small quantities available on a daily basis.

GREAT
GOOD
A CHALLENGE
DODGY
CAUTION

Destination Realities   "Best Practice" Travel Advice

POLLUTION REALITY
6 on a scale of 1-10
A CHALLENGE

Pollution buildup isn't too bad. A tidy and dusty city due to the dry winters and droughts. Cleansing rains are rare. Economic slump has precarious effects on a city and its efforts to sparkle. Industrial pollution isn't heavy. Cars, trucks and buses create some pollution but generally their uses outweigh their threat to air pollution quality. Attention to good sanitation appears to be an economic challenge.

LANGUAGE
Shona, Ndebele, English
A CHALLENGE

English is recognized as an official language, but most widely spoken are Shona and other city dwellers' languages. Many business and hospitality-oriented establishments have people who converse in English. Be cognizant of different interpretations of your country's English and general English terms used locally. For instance, the word "toilet" is more communicative than "the facilities," the "loo" or the "john." Outside of the urban center, little English is spoken. Learn some Shona words and rely on your resources, guides or hosts.

POLITICAL REALITY
Parliamentary Democracy
CAUTION

Capital: Harare

Turmoil and land reform are coming to a head after 20 years. Social order in the city and across many areas of the country are disturbed and affected. Clashes of groups are sporadic and localized, generally not involving international visitors. The government and economy are not stable. Unless there are government warnings not to travel because of violence and very unstable conditions, you may still be able to enjoy some of the wonders of this lovely country.

ECONOMIC REALITY
5 on a scale of 1-10
DODGY

For locals: Life is tough and economic stability has not come to realization as promised. High inflation creates a great burden on the population and its political, social and cultural infrastructures. For tourists: Tourism is a support to the economy and has been developed to bring in money. Check local situation through resources to keep abreast of the political climate for your anticipated visit. Try the Zimbabwe Independent online at **www.samara.co.zw.zimin**.

AIRPORT FACILITIES
Airport Code: HRE
City Code: HRE
A CHALLENGE

Other Airports:
Bulawayo
Victoria Falls

☛ **URBAN CTR**
8 miles
25 - 45 minutes
$25. USD

☛ ✈ **ALLLOW**
1.5 hrs. check-in
2 hrs. transport

Harare International Airport, Harare. This airport and the country's airline network locally and continent-wide are good. The general transportation infrastructure has been good in the past. Commerce and tourism have grown. The airport has not been upgraded to accommodate increased usage and needed passenger amenities. Check the Toursim Office or international airlines flying there: AZ, SR, NW, BA.

BE POLITE: *Listen and observe.*

HAVE MANNERS: *Dress and behave as others around you.*

SHOW INTEREST: *Leave your ego behind, ask questions diplomatically.*

MAKE AN EFFORT: *Fit in. Interact. Engage.*

BE POLITE
Politeness is expected. The British colonial influence remains as a basis for civil communications and interaction. Use professional titles and be respectful. International business has been a basis for economic growth.

HAVE MANNERS
A 2-handed clasped handshake is often the conventional professional greeting for commerce and introductions. Zimbabweans wear Western-style clothes and proudly wear traditional and local dress or celebratory costumes on special occasions. Many personal gestures you possess may be misinterpreted, misunderstood or ignored. Pay attention to authorities and warnings; limit picture-taking to tourist attractions.

SHOW INTEREST
Zimbabweans are hospitable and cautious. Show interest in arts and cultural customs. Local and rural eating customs may involve using your fingers. Participate with interest. Lifestyle is more formal in urban and tourism areas, less formal and very relaxed in rural areas. Direct eye contact and staring, especially of the opposite gender, is considered rude.

MAKE AN EFFORT
Take the time to review the history of the last 20-30 years and how it has impacted the social growth and prosperity of the city and country. Avoid conversations addressing problems with economic, racial and political issues. Be sensitive to current standards that may not be up to your expectations. Topics of interest are international affairs in general, the local industry, arts and sports, like soccer, golf and rugby.

10 Highly Effective Words to "Get By"

1. **A Greeting**	mho-ROH-EE	mhoroi
2. **Please**	Nda-POH-ta	ndapota
3. **Thank You**	ta-TE-nda/ma-ZVI-ta	tatenda/mazvita
4. **Yes**	e-HAY	ehe
5. **No**	I-wah	aiwa
6. **Toilet**	TO-E-re-TEE	toireti
7. **How Much**	E-ma-REE	Imarii
8. **Help**	ndee-ba-TSEE-re-E	ndibatsirei
9. **Excuse Me**	PAM-soh-roh-EE	pamusoroi
10. **Police**	ma-POO-REE-sa	mapurisa

Great Connections & Community

Jot down important phone numbers, contacts, addresses. Great shops and restaurants---get their Email and Web Address.
SCRIBBLE NOTES and info before, during and after!

Airport & Airline Update

Harare Int'l Airport
www.airport-technologies.com/projects/harare_expansion
Current updates limited and not accessible online. This site had general information on expansion projects on the table. Local and global issues are affecting progress.

Air Zimbabwe   **www.airzimbabwe.com**
Airline site not functioning at this time. Check for airline information through a travel industry partner or agent specializing in Africa.

Zimbabwe Tourism   **www.zimbabwe.net/tourism/info**
Funds and resources are forcing Zimbabwe information sites to close down. Limited online tourism information at this time.

Moving Forward Advisory: Stability is unpredictable with limited advisories or current local airport and airline information. Caution advised for travel to this country. Check your local government advisories for travel warnings and updates.

TEAR out & TAKE

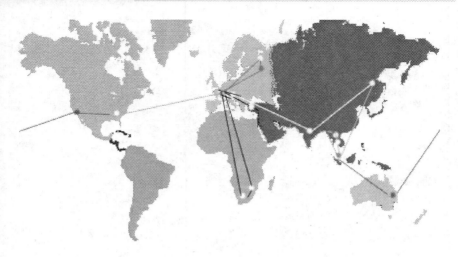

GREAT
GOOD
A CHALLENGE
DODGY
CAUTION

Personal Space
A CHALLENGE

Toilets
GOOD

Cleanliness & Bugs
DODGY

PEOPLE SPACE &
PERSPIRATION

Generally living and driving conditions are dense with people. Sweating is a way of natural life. Limited and/or costly safe water and sanitation diminish urgency and obsessive attention to being clean and crispy every minute---a Western thing. You will blend in and enjoy yourself more if you relax and maintain a more easy going travel style.

TOILETS &
TRIBULATIONS

Western-style toilets were popular and plentiful most of the time. Varying degrees of cleanliness and sanitation were the norm. Always carry a swatch of toilet paper. I carried a roll of toilet paper as a standard travelling necessity; it comes in handy for all kinds of situations, not the least as a travel amenity of choice in toilets around the world.

Toilets and toilet stops were more than adequate when travelling by train and bus.

HYGIENE &
HIGH JINKS

Keep eyes open and be aware of your surroundings. Many health risks, including AIDS. Visit a travel health center before you travel and take suggested health and safety precautions. You don't want malaria! Keep any opportunity for sickness to a minimum. This means watching what you eat. Use bottled water for all normal hygiene rituals you would ordinarily use tap water for. Keep unsanitized water (including shower water) out of eyes, nose and mouth as best practice. Remembering to do this will be to your healthy advantage.

BUGS:

All kinds of wonderful and not so wonderful creatures, like snakes, in my humble opinion, are about. Your level of accommodation usually dictates the level of attention given to keeping out creatures that may disturb urban Westerners.

Western Style

and everything
inbetween

Asian Style

Toilet Stories...

ZIMBABWE

The upmarket Victoria Falls stay at the Rainbow Hotel proved to be a luxury. Hot water, complete bath, toilet and lounging room with mirrors, hairdryer and air conditioning to boot. CNN, big comfy double beds and all the hot water you could soak in. The budget urban experience (budget accommodations---a former resort) on the outskirts of Harare was a deal with trade-offs. The room dubbed the "honeymoon suite" was dated but did sport a long tub. The water, however, was dark brown and NOT inviting. A move to another room offered working toilets with hit or miss (usually miss) hot water and shower stalls. This arrangement was limited on tidy "toilets" but the home-cooked dinner at $3.50 and a welcomed fireplace were balancing amenities. This is where the travel technique E&DS (Eating & Drinking Strategically) started to develop.

Hungary

Hungary
Budapest & Environs

The hills of Buda overlook the once fertile valley of the Danube, now the business pedestrian center of Pest. The Danube snakes through the divide with ornate bridges attaching Buda and Pest. Reminiscent of a Paris before invading Americanism, the former Eastern bloc country bustles with commerce, shops, grand boulevards and some remaining rich architecture, inciting desire to see all.

DISCOVERIES

■ *A huge, modern city with paths to the past cultural and intellectual hangouts.*
■ *Preserved historical areas, easily accessible by tram, bus or train.*
■ *Budapest is proud and its people reflect this with the pace of a new Central Europe. Internet access discovered and connected.*
■ *A visit to a graveyard for old communist era statues by bus through urban and suburban neighborhoods reveals life outside of the big city. On the outskirts of town, a developing neighborhood showcases an outdoor tourist site with huge (10 feet high)* statues of Stalin in bronze, a collection of era heroes in pompous dominion reign. Communist "period" music on a small tape recorder drifts through the air as I model the statue figures, a mere 16th of the size.
■ *Haircuts are cheap and an interpreter helps if you expect your cut to resemble something other than a groovy cut from the 70s'.*
■ *The hot pink open-air tourist bus, instantly renamed the Barbie Bus, threads through the city for a quick overview. It offers an opportunity to catch a tan at the same time.*
■ *Goulash, and Tokaj---Hungarian nectar.*

MAGICAL MOMENTS

■ *Opting to go with the offer of a university dorm for $10.00 a night by a clean-cut English-speaking student at the train station. It proved to be a great choice for economical private accommodations in a big city.*
■ *Hopping the trams to get around with* ease, taking in the architecture, and napping in Margit Syirget Park.
■ *Peeking into courtyards down narrow streets to glean life beyond the rush of buses and people in transit.*
■ *Sitting in the famed Art Nouveau New York Palace Kave listening to a pianist playing classics while he also read the newspaper.*

Destination Realities

"Best Practice" Travel Advice

POPULATION

2 - 2.5 million
`GOOD`

A bustling city well-equipped and practiced at hosting visitors from around the world. Arts and cultural programs are plentiful with a helpful Tourist Office for direction and insight. The city's ease to get around on public transportation soothes the independent and savvy traveller into a comfortable state of being in a short period of time. The urban-centric population nurtures Old World charm and creates a new Central Europe with flare. An easy city to get to know in 2 to 3 days. Worldly and world class.

WEATHER

4 seasons, best off-season
`GOOD`

Budapest is located in Central Europe. Hungary is a landlocked country offering diverse rich hills, fertile valleys, lake resorts and charming villages. Visiting in the spring and fall is preferred, with many activities for locals and visitors to enjoy. Summer is hot and congested. Most locals head to a resort and leave the city during the country's vacationing months of July and August.

TRANSPORT

1st walk, 2nd tram/taxi
`GOOD`

Airport - Repuloter
Train - Vonat
Bus - Busz
Subway - Metro
Taxi - Taxi
Where is - hol van

Trams run consistently and extensively throughout the city. It's relatively easy to check maps and get tickets at a newsstand or metro station (not on the tram). Maps of any sort come in handy to use when asking questions in your few words of Hungarian or English. Traffic in the city is congested and parking is a problem, as in most European cities. Taxis are available at taxi stands and/or on call. Subway transport is available but above-ground travel is more enjoyable in this city unless it is the cold of winter.

PEDESTRIAN-FRIENDLY

8 on a scale of 1-10
`GOOD`

Budapest is an expansive city who's center has been established for centuries. Architecture of Renaissance, Gothic and Art Nouveau persuasions grew into a city center around and over the Danube River that snakes through the country. Turning off the grand boulevards on the Pest side will find you among residential neighborhoods and shops. A village lifestyle flavors the city life and makes Budapest a very pedestrian-friendly, visitor-friendly city.

MONEY

Hungarian FORINT (HUF)
`GOOD`

A new member of the EU (Economic Union), Hungary has been evolving into a competitive free market economy since 1991. Exchange is good value for Hungarian, Central and European products and services. Markets, dining and shopping are great values.

Destination Realities   "Best Practice" Travel Advice

GREAT
GOOD
A CHALLENGE
DODGY
CAUTION

POLLUTION REALITY
7 on a scale of 1-10
A CHALLENGE

Geographically the city and its modern-day pollution are blessed with open space and a river uniting the two former village centers of Buda and Pest. Modern cars, buses and industry are now apparent with a mix of clouds and big-city grit that is common in central European cities. A recent implementation of lead restrictions on gasoline and modified cars have had a positive impact. Older public works and old housing infrastructure has been challenged with a growing and more materialistic generation.

LANGUAGE
Hungarian/Magyar
A CHALLENGE

Magyar, also known more commonly outside of local circles as Hungarian, is a unique language to the people of Hungary. The language is uncompromising to outsiders, with roots in the Fin-Ugric family. People are proud of their country, Magyar history and language. It benefits a non-Hungarian speaker to take time to use the resources available and learn a few words to communicate. It will make a big difference in the willingness and effort on the part of the locals to engage, assist and even speak English.

POLITICAL REALITY
Multiparty Republic
GOOD

Capital: Budapest

A prime minister is the head of the government. Hungary use to be part of the Austro-Hungarian Empire. In the late 80s' it made the transition from a communist state to a relatively stable democratic state. Political change followed to capitalize on a new manufacturing industry. The initial focus on production was established while under a communist state, bordering Russia.

ECONOMIC REALITY
6 on a scale of 1-10
A CHALLENGE

Budapest champions a new, competitive free-market economy since 1991. Being a former communist state has residual influence and power over several generations. Freedom to make choices is new and seems burdensome for a new economic reality. Enterprising commerce and new industrial market development have been growing the economic base slowly. Export of goods and services is growing in the manufacturing industry while privatization programs flourish across select industry sectors.

AIRPORT FACILITIES
Airport Code: BUD
City Code: BUD
GOOD

Other Airports:
check local charters at airport

☛ URBAN CTR
22 miles
30 - 45 minutes
$5 - 15 USD

☛ ✈ ALLOW
2 hrs. check-in
2 hrs. transport

Ferihegy International Airport, Budapest. There are airport changes/upgrades in progress. Terminal 2-B is business and international-oriented. Amenities and shops include a florist, duty free, limited hours of banking/exchange, a staffed tourist center and post office. Check LRI Airport Desk for transport to city. Visit **www.malev.hu** for airport information.

BE POLITE: *Listen and observe.*

HAVE MANNERS: *Dress and behave as others around you.*

SHOW INTEREST: *Leave your ego behind, ask questions diplomatically.*

MAKE AN EFFORT: *Fit in. Interact. Engage.*

BE POLITE ·

Be aware of customs. More conservative behavior is expected and many times indicated by a man's lead. Respect for the individual and the group is expected. Individual small gifts that are given as a token of appreciation are well received... only if there are enough to go around.

HAVE MANNERS

A handshake is an accepted general greeting gesture. Time is strictly adhered to and punctuality is a sign of professionalism and respect. The urban population is a mix of traditional and new pop culture. Men tend to dress more conservatively. The urban young and women tend to express themselves through their selection of dress with style, variety and colors. Err on the conservative side.

SHOW INTEREST

Central Europe has been recognized as an intellectual center in centuries past. A communist state diminished this focus for several generations. New opportunities and openness have flourished. Take interest in industrial development, vineyards and wine making and Hungarian contributions to the global economy, arts and culture.

MAKE AN EFFORT

Learning about what the city environs and people have to offer is essential to orienting yourself and feeling a part of the city. Hungarian people have a proud and not-so-proud recent past which has affected the general populace. Influences of diverse ethnic makeup of neighboring groups is now established as uniquely Hungarian. Wine, new technology and entertainment are good topics of conversation.

10 Highly Effective Words to "Get By"

1. A Greeting	yo-na-POT	jo napot
2. Please	KEH-rem	kerem
3. Thank You	keu-seu-neu-m	koszonom
4. Yes	ee-gen	Igen
5. No	Nehm	nem
6. Toilet	mosh-doh	mosdo
7. How Much	MEH-ni-beh keh-Rool	mennyibe kerul
8. Help	SHAY-gee-tay	segit
9. Excuse Me	bow-CHA-nat	bocsanat
10. Police	ren-deur-sheg	rendorseg

Great Connections & Community

Jot down important phone numbers, contacts, addresses. Great shops and restaurants---get their Email and Web address.
SCRIBBLE NOTES and info before, during and after!

Airport & Airline Update

Budapest Int'l Airport   www.budapest-airport.lri.hu/english
A new and comprehensive information site with daily arrival and departure schedules. Best viewed in Internet Explorer browser. No current passenger advisories posted. Current airport phone contacts listed in news section for direct contact.

Malev Hungarian Airlines   www.malev.hu/english
A comprehensive information site with current advisories to ticketed passengers. The Malev Help Service lists contact for passenger concerns online and on site. Check the site for contact and services.

HNTO-Hungarian National Tourism Office
www.hungarytourism.hu/anglo12
Fresh tourism information and a comprehensive site. No advisories.

Moving Forward Advisory: Budget more time for airport check-in. Your airline site and contact will have most recent information and passenger advice for departure procedures. Expect more time-consuming measures; language may hinder your understanding.

TEAR out & TAKE

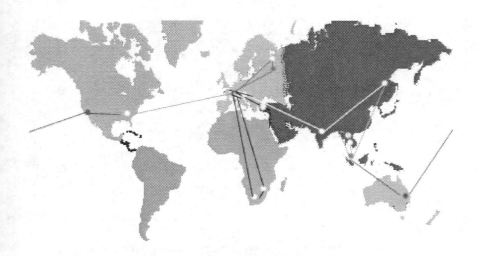

GREAT
GOOD
A CHALLENGE
DODGY
CAUTION

Personal Space
A CHALLENGE

Toilets
GOOD

Cleanliness & Bugs
GOOD

PEOPLE SPACE & PERSPIRATION

Though tight living quarters and a shortage of inexpensive housing has fostered a congenial closeness between family and friends, Hungarians respect a bubble of private space between each other. Public displays of affection and smooching are generally unacceptable, though young generations test social acceptance. Conventions of etiquette should be noted.

An understanding of the cost of hot water and electricity should help you live with these varying standards of hygiene and personal space.

Public transport can get anxiously crowded at times. Be respectful of another's personal space.

TOILETS & TRIBULATIONS

Obsession with cleanliness and beautiful bathrooms are not apparent as with some countries where Western influence has created an obsession for big bathrooms. Avoid public toilets and opt to visit an upscale establishment for coffee or a bite to eat. Carry toilet paper and use sparingly with older plumbing in some areas.

HYGIENE & HIGH JINKS

More relaxed hygiene habits may be noticeable to the squeaky clean high standards of many Westerners. The cost of hot water and electricity limits the luxury of bathing anytime. Bottled water is available and should be used as a preference. The faucet water was safe for general hygiene.

BUGS:

I didn't notice any bugs to be especially concerned about. Mosquitoes abound in the summer season.

Western Style

Asian Style

and everything
inbetween

Toilet Stories...

BUDAPEST

Some cavernous, barely-lit restaurant stops proved to have dingy, untidy toilets. Toilet adventurers beware of dark lighting and dodgy toilets to match.

The university dorm accommodation I stayed in was practically empty and my room was just a few doors down from the "community female bath/toilet" room. The shower was a bit of a trick to work, a big cement-like space, no hooks, but it did the job. I tried to limit any trips at night. My cynical terror-laden imagination did float images of Alfred Hitchcock's *Psycho* inducing pangs of anxiety on my night journeys to the toilet until I safely returned. I now carry a small credit-card-sized flashlight.

Czech Republic

Czech Republic

Prague & Environs

*"The Prague," as **Ivan** says, is stunning. Late sunset and warmth paints the view from the Monastery on the hilltop, a medieval, bridge-clad city scene straight from a fairytale book. Walking for hours across bridges, textured stone paths and side streets. Karlovy Vary Baths, countryside, grilled trout, fresh Gumbrinus beer and a coup de Bechorovcka--- medicinal spirits---freed the mind.*

DISCOVERIES

■ Ivan, a businessman and host extraordinaire, introduced the city and his neighborhood east of the city within minutes of arrival.

■ Dachas, lovely houses, properties and estates taken over by the communist regime are scattered around the country.

■ A remarkable resilience and entrepreneurship is revealed in a citizenship quickly returned to prosperity through perseverance.

■ Internet access in an upscale media and theatre center. Very trendy and edgy.

■ Encountered a former colleague who relocated and opened a successful business in Prague. I congratulate you, "closing the distance - Go Jana!"

■ Times were tough during occupation. No creative thoughts, ideas or actions were allowed. During this time Ivan managed to keep his mind sharp and positioned himself as vice president for a university basketball team. Great stories of travelling around for competitions and entertainment. Very enlightening and image-provoking, creating a sense of the times past.

MAGICAL MOMENTS

■ Dancing in a grand palace courtyard with a violinist's music drifting through the air at sunset. Nobody around but us late, visiting dreamers.

■ Prague castles, Romanesque fortresses circa 1230, and the St. Nicholas, a lovely Czech baroque-style church.

■ Trinkets, jewels, sparkling crystal and lace are just a few treasures to "engage" the wallet while walking along cobblestone streets.

■ Pockets of urban living, gardens and courtyards draw in the curious traveller.

Destination Realities

"Best Practice" Travel Advice

POPULATION
1.2 million
GREAT

There is a refreshing mix of newness and renovation prompted by an invigorated new urban focus and population. Forty years of intellectual and creative oppression hard-wired many. The fast and demanding pace of change is not something older Czechs are interested in. Check the Tourist Office or hotel concierges for advice and recommendations. A little jewel of a Central European city that offers world-class culture, cuisine and commerce. Easy to maneuver, pedestrian-and-transport friendly. 1 to 2 days to ease in. Progressive and world class.

WEATHER
4 seasons, off season-best
GOOD

Off-season allows for the best travel times and prices. Summer or high season may have exceptionally hot spells and many accommodations and cars don't use A/C. Rain doesn't dampen the city or its pace. A river through the city makes it beautiful. Business and life collide in this picturesque bustling city every day. You'll discover your preferred season to visit for business, pleasure and a little bit of both.

TRANSPORT
1st walk, 2nd tram/taxi
GOOD

Airport - letis te
Train - vlak
Bus - autobus
Subway - metro
Taxi - taxi
Where is - kde je

There is good infrastructure for moving people in this compact, pedestrian-friendly city. Citywide bus and tram networks are good but reading signage and instructions are more difficult because of the language. Hailed taxis cost more than ordered taxis and rates vary. It's a tourist-supported city and this "service" will cost. It may be worth the extra cost to "make your day." The train system and tours are recommended. People didn't own their time in the recent past so self-scheduled life is new. Anticipate delays and transport interruptions.

PEDESTRIAN-FRIENDLY
9 on a scale of 1-10
GREAT

Modern traffic is on the increase, but this city is compact and offers all kinds of narrow off-the-tourist-path discoveries. Textured stone paths and streets comfort the visitor with a feeling of history. Pickpockets and street thieves watch for tourists. Walking around with shopping bags of stuff is not recommended. Be cautious of your surroundings. A "fanny pack" is an easy target, it screams "tourist" and thieves know that's where ALL the goods are. Be wise and the wonders of the city will be revealed.

MONEY
KORUNA (CZK)
GOOD

Exchange is best in country for travelers' checks and credit card charges. Having some cash exchanged in advance is always recommended to avoid lines at the airport or to be prepared to take a taxi if other arrangements aren't made or don't show. Central European exchange offers good value for money on most goods and services. Credit cards are widely accepted in upscale business establishments, restaurants and hotels. ATMs are available and so are banks with signs in English for exchange.

GREAT
GOOD
A CHALLENGE
DODGY
CAUTION

Destination Realities | "Best Practice" Travel Advice

POLLUTION REALITY
8 on a scale of 1-10
GOOD

Landlocked, with a river through it, Prague offers canals and bridges and maintains open spaces. Environmental issues are on the agenda as awareness grows that modern pollutants are starting to contribute to building deterioration and low levels of smog in the city. The weather conditions can exacerbate pollution levels and your sensitivity to them. Prague enjoys a relatively low pollution buildup and streets are kept clean as compared to many pedestrian-intense cities.

LANGUAGE
Czech
A CHALLENGE

Czech, a Slavic language, is the official language of the recently formed Czech Republic. German is the most widely spoken language to communicate with visitors. English, while popular with the young and used some in business and hospitality-related situations, is not widely spoken. Signage and print communications are a challenge to interpret. A hired guide and a language cheat sheet are useful to communicate with the people who live here. Tourism efforts are attentive to English-speaking visitors.

POLITICAL REALITY
Parliamentary Democracy
A CHALLENGE

Capital: Prague

The Czech Republic is a developing multiparty parliamentary democracy. The prime minister is the head of government. The president is chief of state. Privatization and new economic pressures have changed the landscape of politics since the communist regime ended and independence began in 1997. Diverse parties are in flux, drawing attention to regional, private and party-line issues. Listen to current affairs and local issues at **www.radio.cz/english**.

ECONOMIC REALITY
7 on a scale of 1-10
GOOD

For many, creating wealth, as an individual, business, or nation, was a concept that was all but extinguished during the communist regime. Prague, since the 1990s, has been undergoing rapid social and economic change. Business interests and reforms, with attention to tourism, find economic stability quickly approaching the scale of a comparable Western city. Goods and services are plentiful in the city and other urban areas. Anticipate limited and less-reliable goods and services in rural areas.

AIRPORT FACILITIES
Airport Code: PRG
City Code: PRG
GOOD

Other Airports:
Pardubice
Brno
Karlovy Vary

☛ URBAN CTR
12 miles
20 - 60 minutes
$13.50 - 20.00 USD
☛ ✈ ALLOW
1.5 hrs. check-in
1 hrs. transport

Ruzyne International Airport, Prague. Cedaz minibus shuttle to Old Town Center--- inexpensive. Taxi may be up to 600 CZK. Airport contact number: 420 22011 3321. Many amenities are available, including convenient transport, a post office, shopping and travel-related information. Internet kiosks available in transit area and business lounges. The airport authority Website is in Czech only. A good alternative is: **www.praguesite.cz**.

BE POLITE: *Listen and observe.*

HAVE MANNERS: *Dress and behave as others around you.*

SHOW INTEREST: *Leave your ego behind, ask questions diplomatically.*

MAKE AN EFFORT: *Fit in. Interact. Engage.*

BE POLITE

Central Europeans have a history of "civilized" influences collected over the centuries from great courts, kings, and wars to communist rule. Communist proletariat rule oppressed traditional customary courtesies. Politeness is natural and expected in all situations regardless of one's lack of enthusiasm to return the same.

HAVE MANNERS

Observe and reflect on the urban mix of people and their lifestyles and age. Respect for elders is a given and respect for everyone is expected. Western mannerisms may be misinterpreted. Keep flashy Western lifestyle to a minimum and pay attention to resorting to a more reserved business and social manner. The Czech young people are more multicultural, multilingual and freer in their ways of communicating than many of their parents. This freedom may be revealed through trendy dress, design, art and business acumen.

SHOW INTEREST

The Czech Republic has emerged through civil and social disruption to blossom as an independent nation. It has taken great spirit, courage and patience. Take interest in their history, accomplishments and current issues affecting their struggle for continued independence and freedom.

MAKE AN EFFORT

This region has been affected by immigration, dispossession and political issues that continue today. Rapid change and Westernization isn't necessarily seen as progress or the best way by many. Current affairs and old historical topics will engage different people based on their experience. Listen and you will learn much.

10 Highly Effective Words to "Get By"

1. A Greeting	do-BRI den or AH-hawy	dobry den or ahoj
2. Please	pro-SEEM	prosim
3. Thank You	de-KOO-ye-vam	de kuji vam
4. Yes	AH-no	ano
5. No	nay	ne
6. Toilet	twa-LEH-ta	toaleta
7. How Much	kaw-LEEK-taws-to-EE	kolik to stoji
8. Help	POH-maw-tchi	pomoci
9. Excuse Me	proh-mi-ni-TEH	prominite
10. Police	paw-leet-ZEE-e	policie

Great Connections & Community

Jot down important phone numbers, contacts, addresses. Great shops and restaurants---get their Email and Web Address. **SCRIBBLE NOTES** and info before, during and after!

Airport & Airline Update

Prague Int'l Airport   **www.csl.cz/en**
A new updated site. Comprehensive English version with passenger departure recommendations. Don't carry knives; limited cabin baggage enforced. Look here for future advisories.

Czech Airlines   **www.csa.cz/en**
A comprehensive information, service and online booking site. Look for advisories in the future.

Prague Tourism Bureau   **www.parguetourism.org**
Developing site with visitor information. Updates sporadic.

Moving Forward Advisory: Budget 1.5 to 2 hours for airport check-in. No new measures are communicated online, however all major airports and airlines are trying to accommodate new procedures and ensure passenger safety. Anticipate delays and rescheduling. Check online and offline with direct airline contacts in advance.

TEAR out & TAKE

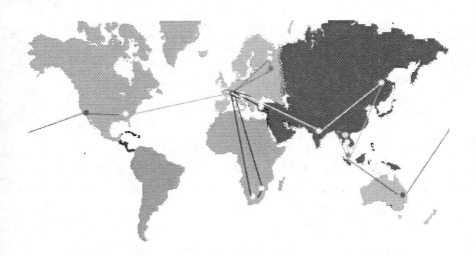

GREAT
GOOD
A CHALLENGE
DODGY
CAUTION

Personal Space
GOOD

Toilets
GOOD

Cleanliness & Bugs
GOOD

PEOPLE SPACE & PERSPIRATION

A pedestrian-dense city with neighborhoods and pockets of families who have been around for decades. Public transport is good and public utilities are old in most cases. Air conditioning is costly and not generally available. You and everyone who lives here endures the hot spells and utility dysfunctions whenever they arise.

TOILETS & TRIBULATIONS

Western standards apply with general upkeep of public toilets on the negligible side. Private toilets in hotels and restaurants vary in amenities and cleanliness. Most are generally in line with the level or status of the establishment. No big surprises or toilet terrors here.

HYGIENE & HIGH JINKS

This city seemed clean and tidy. Well-established patterns of life keep everything and everybody in place. A temperate climate also helps the appearance and upkeep of establishments and the environs.

BUGS:

I didn't notice any. City dwellings vary and so do an accommodation's attention to any possible bug problems.

Western Style

and everything
inbetween

Asian Style

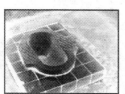

Toilet Stories...

PRAGUE

No toilet troubles here. Toilets were plentiful, manageable and tolerable, albeit a bit dingy and not well lit. No worries across the board. Many quaint establishments had tiny, quaint toilets to match. Some restaurant toilets have co-ed toilets and (general public) one-sink wash basins. No amenities or space for primping or lounging. Do your business and move on quickly is best practice. And always carry a swatch or two of toilet paper. It comes in handy.

Turkey

Turkey
Istanbul & Environs

MEMORIES

Byzantine domes, tasselled tea pots and dazzling pillows mix with floating chants of prayer and courageous cars at every corner. Modern and ancient cultures balance and evolve scorching visual impressions of life into memory. The heart and bowels of civilization and East meets West. Fresh fish, mosques, a young guide named **Yelchen** *and tapestries. Would you like some apple tea?*

DISCOVERIES

■ Negotiating and barter skills are challenged, improved upon or put to shame.

■ The epitome of salesmanship and relationship building. A call to purchase behind every smile mixed with merchant ritual and Turkish hospitality demands participation and engagement. Life is business and business is life.

■ Food is life. An agriculturally rich country with diverse climate and geography offers succulent, perfect peaches, to die for tomatoes and bigger than your head slabs of fresh feta. Diverse and colorful cuisine.

■ Turkish people pay cash for everything including their housing. It is not unusual to see people going in and out of banks with brown bags of money.

■ Carpet merchants, even if they are travel agents, businessmen and tour guides, take their profession seriously. Shop around, negotiate and if you engage in a counter offer---you're considered a committed buyer. Variety and price are better outside the major cities. Standards in business practice vary also. Don't leave Turkey without a magic carpet.

MAGICAL MOMENTS

■ Finding a reasonably priced $75.00 hotel room upon arrival in Ataturk International Airport at 12:45 a.m. on a Saturday night. The airport was teaming with families, action and sweat.

■ Meeting a young tour guide, **Yelchen**, who introduced us to apple tea, carpets,

his two sweet sisters and uncle from Urfa and the best kabobs in the city. Touring the city on foot, by boat and car offered multiple perspectives and revealed enchanting realities.

■ Walking the streets in the evening was wonderful. It's safe but be aware.

Destination Realities

"Best Practice" Travel Advice

POPULATION
9 million plus
A CHALLENGE

Best practice in a city of 9 million plus is to use the visitor resources available. This saves time and helps you find what you desire faster. Check the Tourist Office or hotel concierges for advice and recommendations; airlines are good sources also. Istanbul is over 3,000 years old and continues to serve visitors from around the world. Take city tours, check guide books and use a map. A world class city, 2 to 3 days to ease in.

WEATHER
4 seasons, long summer
GREAT

Weather is diverse across the country, but the most visited western coastal sections and cities are generally dry and warm. Short, cold winters with much rain. Long, dry spring and summer. Business as usual in the winter but visitors frequent mainly during the other 3 seasons. Most places don't have A/C, so if visiting in the summer season expect to sweat and expect business attire to be more on the casual side. Cars generally don't have or use air conditioning.

TRANSPORT
1st walk, 2nd taxi
GOOD

Airport - havaalanz
Train - trein
Bus - otobyus
Subway - metro
Taxi - taxi
Where is - herede

In the city, buses, ferries and boats are common modes of transportation. Dolmus (small buses) shuttle between suburbs and cities. Taxis are reasonable and plentiful, but traffic is unpredictable and overcrowded. Public transport is plentiful and well-used. Best practice is to take a map, allow walk time and use public transport. Ask at your hotel for help or advice on transport and the best way to get from A to B.

PEDESTRIAN-FRIENDLY
8 on a scale of 1-10
GOOD

Modern traffic hovers above the byzantine maze of streets and convenient squares. The cars have the right of way but are in the minority. Walking is efficient, visually stimulating and safe. Watch where you're going. It takes time and, weather permitting, walking is how everyone gets from A to B with a quick hop on a bus and/or boat. Safety in numbers when walking is always advisable. Feel free to attach yourself to a safe-looking couple if you feel uncomfortable or stop in a shop or hotel to regain your direction or recommendations for a safe route.

MONEY
LIRA (TRL)
GOOD

Exchange is best "in country" for travelers' checks. Having some cash exchanged in advance is always recommended to avoid lines at the airport or to be prepared to take a taxi if other arrangements aren't made or don't show. Good value for money. Use cash (LIRA) for daily expenses. Credit cards are widely accepted in most business establishments, restaurants and hotels. ATMs are plentiful and so are banks noted with signs in English for exchange.

Destination Realities   "Best Practice" Travel Advice

POLLUTION REALITY
6 on a scale of 1-10
DODGY

Pollution build-up is common in large cities of 3-5 million; imagine 9 million. A general gray soot and dust are noticeable just about any time. Depending on where you are coming from, you'll notice it right away. Be advised: 21st-century traffic is growing and causing more pollution to the city air. Hot and steamy summers are the worst. Avoid midday, relax in a non-congested area and plan to endure it. You'll get used to it, live with it and go on about your business.

LANGUAGE
Turkish & dialects
A CHALLENGE

Travel and hospitality industry professionals usually have a good command of English. City folks are busy yet usually very hospitable. Humble travellers requesting help will generally find city folks helpful, and though they may not be able to speak English, they will try to help and communicate in what they do know. Be understanding if they do not have time to figure out what you are trying to say. Don't take it personally. Try a shop or hotel for assistance.

POLITICAL REALITY
Republic
A CHALLENGE

Capital: Ankara

Turkish Republic. Political change is volatile and tested. West more open and progressive to Western ways. East tends to retain hold on tradition and more singular religious values. Regional eruptions of civil and national conflicts should be paid attention to. Your nationality alone may place you in uncomfortable situations that you should be aware of. Maintain a low profile. Keep distinguishing national outward appearances and mannerisms to a minimum. Heed alerts and warnings.

ECONOMIC REALITY
8 on a scale of 1-10
GOOD

For Locals: Life is broadening for the upper and middle classes, with rural folks making do. For Visitors: The city is bustling in goods, services and amenities to attract Western visitors for business and pleasure. Tourism and exports are strong economic factors supporting the city so you will notice someone at every shop calling your attention to buy-buy-buy at every opportunity. Straight purchases are expected from visitors and bargaining is a way of life for the locals and savvy tourists.

AIRPORT FACILITIES
Airport Code: ATK
City Code: IST
GREAT

Other Airports:
Izmir
Ankara

☛ **URBAN CTR**
24 miles
35 - 60 minutes
$25. USD

☛ ✈ **ALLOW**
1.5 hrs. check-in
3 hrs. transport

Ataturk International Airport, Istanbul. Millennium ready, the new international airport accommodates 14 million passengers annually. Great amenities for the international traveller, including the necessary and extras like a post office, meeting rooms and a conference lounge. Check **www.AtaturkAirport.com** *to get a glimpse and ask questions via Email. Telephone +90 244.285.20.21.*

BE POLITE: *Listen and observe.*

HAVE MANNERS: *Dress and behave as others around you.*

SHOW INTEREST: *Leave your ego behind, ask questions diplomatically.*

MAKE AN EFFORT: *Fit in. Interact. Engage.*

BE POLITE
Be open to rituals of hospitality but cautious of pressure to buy. Observe religious etiquette and adapt dress to city social code. Be cognizant of national pride, tensions and local concerns with anyone you meet along the journey.

HAVE MANNERS
Observe and accept mannerisms. A hand shake is a conventional exchange. Many common North American gestures send mixed signals, so keep a low profile with hand signals and nonverbal communications unless you know how they will be interpreted. Women should dress in loose fitting long pants, skirts and non-revealing shirts. Observe colors worn by city women. A scarf should cover the head in mosques. Be very unintrusive and sport a humble demeanor. Quiet observation is appreciated and considered respectful when visiting mosques. Men may take advantage of unsure, flashy (even not so flashy) foreign-looking, vacationing women. Consideration for their ways results in respect and generally less hassle.

SHOW INTEREST
General - Return hospitality with not too revealing general answers and make evaluations of your time and a merchants intentions. Food---cuisine is a part of life. Try recommended restaurants and selections as advertised. Generally food is more oil based. Beware of your choices of food if you have delicate digestion. Topics---current events, economics and culture mix here. Show interest in economy and concern for Turkish lifestyle and culture in general. Don't be boastful. Take interest in others.

MAKE AN EFFORT
Hospitality is a tradition. Turkish people know how to take care of visitors. Trust genuine hospitality once you get past the touts and hard sellers. Other Turkish folks, just like you, are visiting for business or vacation. Don't be afraid to interact with the people and places you visit.

10 Highly Effective Words to "Get By"

1. A Greeting	MEHR-hah-ba	merhaba
2. Please	LEWT-fehn	lutfen
3. Thank You	CHOHK-teh-shen-KEWR	Cok Teshekkur
4. Yes	eh-VEHT	evet
5. No	HAH-yuhr	hayr
6. Toilet	too-vah-LEHT	fuvalet
7. How Much	KAHCH/tah-neh	Kac/cak tane
8. Help	yahr-DUHM-eh-den	yerim edin
9. Excuse Me	parh-don	pardon
10. Police	poh-LEES	polis

Great Connections & Community

Jot down important phone numbers, contacts, addresses. Great shops and restaurants---get their Email and Web Address. **SCRIBBLE NOTES** and info before, during and after!

Airport & Airline Update

Istanbul Int'l Airport   **www.ataturkairport.com**
A new comprehensive, information and new services-rich site to match the newly renovated airport. Use Internet Explorer browser for English version. Email directly for inquiries.

Turkish Airlines   **www.thy.com**
A new full-featured Website, including online booking and new online check-in services. A news section designated on the homepage should have check-in and media advisories forthcoming.

Ministry of Tourism, Turkey   **www.tourismturkey.org**
A pop-up window quickly addresses a notice regarding the current events. An FAQ page has posted assurances of meeting recently instituted FAA requirements. An excellent resource site.

Moving Forward Advisory: Budget 2 hours for domestic and 3 hours for international departures. In a new, huge airport, it takes time to get oriented and checked in because of attention to procedures. Check online and offline with direct airline contacts in advance. Airport provides many amenities and enhanced services.

T E A R out & T A K E

75

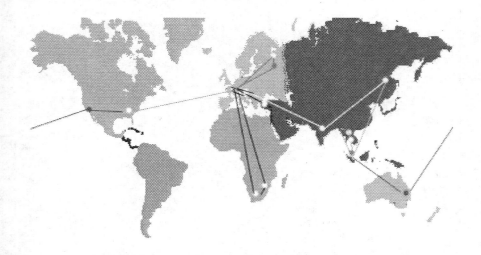

| GREAT |
| GOOD |
| A CHALLENGE |
| DODGY |
| CAUTION |

;-) Earplugs come in handy, especially if you are not used to hearing prayers float through the city from strategically located public loudspeakers between 5:00 and 5:30 a.m.

Personal Space
GOOD

Toilets
DODGY

Cleanliness & Bugs
GOOD

PEOPLE SPACE & PERSPIRATION

An ancient city, and one of wealth and European influence. Busy city life is similar to standard Western, cosmopolitan cities. People are respectful of personal space. Closeness increases with familiarity. Public transportation can be tight and in-your-face with body odors to match.

Crowding is commonplace, especially in high season. The city's population has increased dramatically causing many intrusions on people's personal and private space. Life is rich and engaging, but don't get too distracted by the crowds and people watching, tourist-targeting thieves are keeping an eye for you.

TOILETS & TRIBULATIONS

All variety of toilets with accompanying smells to match, seem...shall we say... a bit dodgy. Top hotels have the nicest facilities with diminishing attention to cleanliness from there. Public toilets are generally Western style. Always carry a swatch or two of toilet paper. Plumbing systems are generally temperamental so use the toilet paper sparingly. In private homes, mid-range and budget hotels the arrangement can be unique with a tiny separate sink/ shower in another room from the toilet. Many floor basins also include a pail and water for flushing. Best practice is don't drink too much liquid and endure public toilets at convenient stops.

HYGIENE & HIGH JINKS

Millions of people and an ancient city spells congestion and pollution with trash here and there. Many jobs are to keep the streets and shop fronts tidy and swept. Generally the city is pretty clean. Again, it depends on where you're coming from. Personal hygiene is much more relaxed. Don't be judgmental; you'll be sweating and feeling the grit of the big city in no time. Hotels, are tidy for the most part, but always check a room before you make a commitment. Restaurants vary in hygiene---be cautious where and what you eat. Drink bottled water and use it when brushing teeth as the best practice.

BUGS:

Bugs exist in all cities, I didn't encounter many mosquitoes here, but the crawling kind are around. Bug spray is readily available.

Western Style

Asian Style

and everything
inbetween

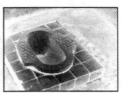

Toilet
Stories...

Datcha, Southern Turkey

I award this bathroom a few stars for the most unique setup. From a Western perspective it's a "bathroom" in the Western sense with a strange twist. Envision a large shower-stall-size bathroom, completely tiled with one handheld showerhead poised above the toilet. A great cleaning tool to hose off...me, the toilet, the sink and every inch of the bathroom. There was no distinction between shower and bathroom, "one big thing" as I tend to exclaim often. I cherished it once I got used to hosing off everything in the bathroom. It was hot and I hosed off several times a day and in the middle of the night. There was no air conditioning.

India

India
Mumbai/Delhi/Rajasthan

MEMORIES

*Mumbai (formerly known as Bombay) CRASH. A carnival-like collage and assault on delicate Western senses. Nature controls life...cows, elephants, monkeys and children...children everywhere. S-m-o-o-t-h, cool marble-floored Jain temples with intricately carved panels. Lime green, saffron yellow scarf-clad ladies, working, walking and busy in life. Toothless **Ali**...tuk-tuk extraordinaire. Mango lass-ies, curry and monsoon rains.*

DISCOVERIES

■ *Rajasthan and great royalty, animal hunts, glitzy palaces and vast kingdoms past are scattered across central and northern India.*
■ *The crush of population and poverty are vibrant, overwhelming and dense in the urban centers.*
■ *Signs and warnings: A warning on a temple advising "You will suffer" if you enter on monthly period - "Do not enter." Another sign--"washing in river prohibited. Watch for crocodiles." For peace of mind, heed ALL warnings.*
■ *Many speak English, this is very helpful. However, communication styles and body language are VERY different from Western communication styles.*
■ *Telephones and roads are unreliable. Get used to it, Internet access and wireless com-munications are on the way, now popping up in villages and towns everywhere.*
■ *Those with red-stained teeth are indulg-ing in a quick energy stimulant (paan).*
■ *Open lands with herds of goats that may be escorted by brightly Sari-clad ladies catch your eye. These vivid colors and textures dot the landscape with life, a contrast to crowds.*
■ *Tolerance is tested by the minute, your humility level is realized and adjusted.*

MAGICAL MOMENTS

■ *Spending hours watching dramatic swatches of clouds pass behind the Taj Mahal, milky marble squares patched together and rounded to form a domed jewel in the middle of chaos and urbanism.*
■ *Dancing across a marble corridor like a princess after a delightful dinner at the magical Lake Palace Hotel, Udaipur.*
■ *Listening to rain and the chanting of Jain practitioners from the Bikaner House --- the palace balcony suite, Mt. Abu.*
■ *Kalpana rooftop restaurant high above traffic (children, animals and tuk-tuks) with a view of Jaisalmer's walled fortress.*

Destination Realities   "Best Practice" Travel Advice

POPULATION
Mumbai-14 mil Delhi-8 mil
DODGY

The crush of the city population, including cows, goats and an elephant or two, is overwhelming to Western visitors. City centers are dense with rural groups looking for employment and opportunity. The majority are poor, displaced and looking to fit in somewhere. Class status remains an intricate component of changing social and economic values and mores. Mumbai and Delhi are powerful commerce and political centers. India has a country population of 1 billion plus. It takes 3 to 5 days to get comfortable.

WEATHER
summery; Oct.-Mar. best
A CHALLENGE

Seasonal changes include a hot unpredictable monsoon-heavy climate. Climate varies across the country with extremes depending on the region. Prepare for heat and intermittent rains. A/C is a luxury afforded by the middle and upper classes and many business and tourist establishments. Electricity is interupted often. Be prepared when walking to deal with weather-driven pockets of pollution, rain and dense, dusty conditions. Electricity is dodgy as is any guarantee of A/C. Mother nature rules - adapt.

TRANSPORT
Hired car/Taxi/Tuk-Tuk
A CHALLENGE

Airport - havai aadaa
Train - rahil
Bus - bus
Subway - bhUmigata rail
Taxi - kerai ke gaadi
Where is - kahan hay

Prepaid taxis are the best bet from airport to city center/hotel. Public infrastructure for transportation is in place and overburdened by dense population. If you're driving or being driven in a hired car, you can easily be stalled in dense, chaotic traffic. Cows and animals own the streets of these cities and have the right-of-way. Tuk-tuks will clamor to serve you. Expect a challenge and hassle. Agree on price and destination. Plan to be delayed along the way with other suggested stops. Trade-offs in time and money include air pollution and children with offerings at stops.

PEDESTRIAN-FRIENDLY
4 on a scale of 1-10
CAUTION

Getting around in these cities is a challenge with a more organic and natural relationship between animals, established public transport and automobiles. Walking is the main mode of transportation, but the city infrastructure doesn't include an obvious plan. The huge city sections are spread out in different areas of the city. While a certain area is pedestrian-friendly and easy to get around in, to get from one area to another usually involves any manner of public transport. Tuk-tuks come in handy to get you to your destination.

MONEY
RUPEE (INR)
A CHALLENGE

Strict currency policy: rupees must stay in the country. Use local cash for needs in small denominations is most useful. Exchange money or travelers' checks at airport or city-authorized exchange kiosks. Beware of too-good-to-be-true-exchange services. Banks are not convenient for quick money exchange. Hotel exchange rates might be higher, but are reliable, usually offering encashment slips suggested to retain as receipts. ATMs are available and credit cards are accepted for big purchases and at many establishments and hotels.

| GREAT |
| GOOD |
| A CHALLENGE |
| DODGY |
| CAUTION |

POLLUTION REALITY
4 on a scale of 1-10
CAUTION

Heavy, hot weather increases the density of pollution. While pollution policies are in place, many cars still use leaded gasoline. Cows and animals included in the city mix add to unsanitary conditions that run off into the water and are easily picked up by people. Contaminated water continues to be of concern for the local population as well as for visitors. Use a handkerchief to cover your mouth if needed and wipe sweat from your face. It's a reality, so handle it and adapt.

LANGUAGE
Hindi and 15 others
GOOD

Diversity-rich, Indians recognize 16 official languages, 700 dialects. English bridges the communications gap in many non-Hindi cross-cultural communications. The aftereffects of British colonial rule and influence color the cultural complexion of communications. English is learned and used in day-to-day commerce and schooling. Hindi is the most widely spoken. Each community and region is proud and protective of its culture and language. Spoken English and accompanying body language take on Indian-specific meaning. Learn to interpret and understand.

POLITICAL REALITY
Multiparty Federal Republic
A CHALLENGE

Capital: New Delhi
Largest City: Mumbai
(Formerly Bombay)

The Congress Party was established 27 years after Britain annexed India. National self-rule and industrialization were advanced through efforts of Mahatma Gandhi and Prime Minister Nehru. Many state-owned companies struggle with growth and independence. Long-established political powers are confronted with changing and challenging groups within India. Political power plays and disputes are ongoing with neighboring countries Pakistan and Kashmir. Stability is relative.

ECONOMIC REALITY
5 on a scale of 1-10
DODGY

From a global view, India is in the top ten big emerging markets. National economic, political and social unity and success have been plagued with deep religious beliefs, disputes and cultural traditions. The 1950s established economic and political agendas,(a license-quota-subsidy-raj), and has been in controll of the economic landscape. A traditional hierarchical and class-conscious culture confronts issues both stimulating and stunting growth. Illiteracy and poverty plague the masses and urbanization challenges stability.

AIRPORT FACILITIES
Airport Code: BOM
City Code: BOM
A CHALLENGE

Other Airports:
Calcutta   Chocin
Delhi   Chennai
Goa

☛ **URBAN CTR**
18 miles
40 - 90 minutes
$8 - 12 USD

☛ ✈ **ALLOW**
2 hrs. check-in
2-3 hrs. transport

Sahar International Airport, Mumbai. A port city and international hub for the Indian subcontinent. Security is tight with attention to passengers and import/export goods. Limited on amenities. Spacious areas to accommodate a chaotic influx of people at all times of the day and night. There is a 24-hour business center. Secure a prepaid taxi to the city. Airport: 22.836.6767 and **www.mumbaiairport.com**.

BE POLITE: *Listen and observe.*

HAVE MANNERS: *Dress and behave as others around you.*

SHOW INTEREST: *Leave your ego behind, ask questions diplomatically.*

MAKE AN EFFORT: *Fit in. Interact. Engage.*

BE POLITE

Gracious and hospitable, Indians are generally open to Westerners. Be conscious of economic and political issues that Westerners tend to complain about. Many Indians respect humble and unmaterialistic attitudes over affluence and Western arrogance. Keep criticism and judgments to yourself.

HAVE MANNERS

Key to understanding relations and social interactions is to know that nature is the controlling factor of life. It's easier to adapt to this seemingly chaotic, organic approach to life when you understand and accept an extended family lifestyle that incorporates home and business. *Namaste* (Na-mahs-TAY) is a congenial and appropriate greeting in most business and social situations. This greeting is accompanied by hands clasped in prayer style with a short bow. A handshake is also appropriate in most business, commerce and social circumstances.

SHOW INTEREST

India's business and social practices are traditional with an appreciation for many Western influences. There's also disappointment in and resentment for many of the commercial and materialistic influences that have infiltrated India. Take interest in new entrepreneurial class and traditions. Avoid topics of common distress regarding economics, environment and politics. Indians, with a growing middle class taking on the world, possess great intellect, diversity and industrial power. India takes on unfathomable social and political challenges every day and will continue to master them to claim a stake in the new global economy.

MAKE AN EFFORT

Leave your Western affluence and arrogance at home. You're a prime target for the less fortunate and for those who prey on tourists. Tolerance and flexibility are key intangible skills to help you in dealing with a world very different from your own. Cultivate an appreciation for the people, culture, history and beauty that make up India.

10 Highly Effective Words to "Get By"

1. A Greeting	Na-mahs-TAY	namaste
2. Please	kriy-PEH-yah	kripyaa
3. Thank You	THAA-nya VAA-t	dhanyavaad
4. Yes	haah	ha
5. No	na-HEE	nahi
6. Toilet	saw-CHAH-lay or Bath-ROON	sauchalya or bathroon
7. How Much	yah-kit-NEH ka hai	yeh kit neh ka hai
8. Help	h-v-re or (come! a-nah)	hvre or (come! ana)
9. Excuse Me	sham-MAH kah-RAY	shamma kare
10. Police	THA-na or pow-LEE-s	thana or police

Great Connections & Community

Jot down important phone numbers, contacts, addresses. Great shops and restaurants---get their Email and Web Address.
SCRIBBLE NOTES and info before, during and after!

Airport & Airline Update

Mumbai Int'l Airport   **www.mumbaiairport.com**
General information site with updates, but not necessarily concerning passenger check-in or media advisories. General airport information. Limited information on improvement plans. Contact page and info links.

Air India   **www.airindia.com**
General information site listing services, offering general flight and inflight information and background. May include advisories in news section in the future.

India Tourist Office   **www.india-tourism.de/english**
A comprehensive general resource. Execllent maps and links to suit most inquiring online needs. Downloadable brochures and info.

Moving Forward Advisory: Online information and communications hard to come by. Look to local carriers and agents for passenger updates and advice. Airport facilities limited on amenities or recent improvements. Anticipate interruptions and rescheduling of flights.

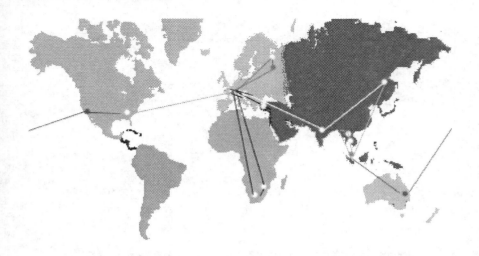

DARE to Travel the World

> *GREAT*
> *GOOD*
> *A CHALLENGE*
> *DODGY*
> *CAUTION*

Personal Space
DODGY

Toilets
DODGY

Cleanliness & Bugs
DODGY

PEOPLE SPACE & PERSPIRATION

Making generalizations is tough because India is so diverse. Due to the influx of rural groups moving to the city, you'll find overcrowding and very, very close encounters. People live in large extended families and groups and do so in small spaces. So there's a lot of sweating! Many have very limited access to water, let alone clean water. Be prepared to sweat with the best and worst of them. Seek out an upmarket hotel or restuarant for a reprieve from the crowds.

TOILETS & TRIBULATIONS

India poses seemingly insurmountable challenges to toilet rituals and expectations. Travelling around is more of a problem because public toilets are few and far between, except in train stations and airports. There are some if you take the RIGHT bus that makes a scheduled stop. Choosing the RIGHT bus is tricky. Ladies wear a long skirt. This offers some coverage should you get stuck on a roadside... that is common. Western establishments offer Western toilets. Train toilets are, at minimum, dodgy. Traditional and rural toilet techniques include using water with the left hand to rinse after you go. Toilet paper clogs in-need-of -repair-plumbing. Where you are dictates your technique.

HYGIENE & HIGH JINKS

The population has far outpaced the infrastructure to meet demands for public works in areas of electricity, sewers and public services. Unsanitary conditions and contaminated water create a health risk at every turn. Drink and carry some quality bottled water. Stick to canned soda and bottled beverages. Be careful what you eat. Stick to fresh-cooked dishes or packaged foods. Watch expiration dates and packaging. Many things are recycled from one place to another. Go to reputable or popular establishments. Pack liquid Pepto Bismol, it's a life saver. Keep towelettes or hankerchief available for washing hands. Use bottled water for face washing and for brushing teeth.

BUGS:

Beware of mosquitos and spiders.

Western Style

Asian Style

and everything
inbetween

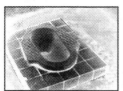

Toilet Stories...

Jaisalmer, India...be on the defensive.

Up at 4:15 a.m. to go through packing and getting-ready-to-travel-on rituals. A successful "movement" was a critical function before the impending 6-hour journey by bus. Departure was 5:40 a.m. Two stops were made. I used the first stop to take a toilet break (good judgment on my part, the 2nd stop---horrors!).

Stop one---I followed two women, each wearing a lovely sari, in hopes they would lead me to toilet facilities. I decided to follow them with the intent to copy what they do. Then I---with some hesitation---followed them around a corner of a building and imitated the toilet-going-rituals of this bus riding group. One at a time, each of us took a squat position, open air against a wall in an open parking lot, a piece of toilet paper in hand. The view...an active truck stop across the way. No blinds to shut, this was it, wide open and available. If these women could do it, I could do it. I had on my long skirt in anticipation of a road-stop-go-in-bush opportunity. This reminded me of concerts past when drinking too much beer would find me in the bushes near...but it was always dark. My toilet tolerance was pushed to a new level and one of my new travel techniques, E&DS (**E**at and **D**rink **S**trategically), was in place, in practice and working.

■ Ask me about clogging up the whole plumbing system at the Bikaner's Palace.

China

China
Beijing & Environs

MEMORIES

Layers of hills, shaded mountains and the Great Wall---8 horse carriages wide---weaves its way through a dynamic landscape. Steam engine soft-sleeper train to Xi'an, ancient capital of China. Temple of Heaven. Grand doors, public works and ancient ingenuity. Thousands of Qin Terra Cotta Warriors and Horses. Street stall noodles, masterful chopsticks, suspicious looks and Peking Duck.

DISCOVERIES

■ *Construction everywhere. Beijing, offering hundreds of sites, museums, antiques and artifacts, is smoggy and spread out.*
■ *Bikes and cars get you from place to place. Bikes, pedicabs and bike-rickshaws rule!*
■ *Clean and tidy in the main squares and general tourist areas, but sections of worn old buildings show wear and tear---a harder urban living existence.*
■ *Great street markets and stalls with all kinds of trinkets, large and small.*
■ *Chinese Daily, an English newspaper, black and red with news to orient a newcomer.*

■ *Internet access was hard to find. The hotel had it, but it wasn't functioning well. Hit or miss in both connectivity and time when to use it.*
■ *Bike-rickshaws of variety and personality. Pick one and negotiate a fare. Language makes this difficult at times.*
■ *Taxis come in 3 levels. Budget is a van of sorts, you hop on and hop off. Cheap, usually dumpy and it gets you there or in the vicinity. The next levels include taxis or hired cars, available for all tastes and wallets. Opt for more costly small taxi or sedan for comfort.*

MAGICAL MOMENTS

■ *With an amazing command of English, our guide, **Lisa**, 22, delivered stories of history. She shared insights about living in urban Beijing. How lives are similar. How they differ.*
■ *A 24-hour train ride to Xi'an, with stops along the way, allowed interesting jumps out to the platform to stretch the legs and*

observe. Memorable views of rural life and farmed fields.
■ *Wide sidewalks dressed haphazardly with card tables and chairs, pails of noodles in stall after stall. Good eating and smiles.*
■ *Dancing and walking along the Fortress of Xi'an, opened for a special occasion.*

Destination Realities

"Best Practice" Travel Advice

POPULATION
Beijing 10 million plus
A CHALLENGE

A country of 1.2 billion people under centralized rule lends some organization to the mass of people. Beijing is sectioned into 3 or 4 areas. Getting from A to B may look easy on a map, but it is quite a distance. This city is a challenge for Westerners because of language, structured tourism (which limits pricing choices), and limited freedom for spontaneous travel. Guides and a guided tour are recommended to work within the dense city and its busy population. It takes 3 to 5 days to get to know. World class.

WEATHER
4 seasons - spring/fall best
A CHALLENGE

Four seasons are the norm with very cold winters and very hot summers in Beijing's city center. Summer is high season and though generally prepared with air conditioning in many establishments and hotels, don't expect A/C in cars and buildings everywhere, especially outside the city. Rain showers are sporadic any season so purchase an umbrella there. A portable raincoat is useful off-season as it tends to cool off at night. A huge city---its population moves no matter what the weather.

TRANSPORT
Walk/Rickshaw//Taxi
A CHALLENGE

Airport - fei-dji-chang
Train - huo che
Bus - gong che
Subway - di tie
Taxi - (chu=qu) qu zu
Where is - zai na li

Everyone is in transit in some form or fashion, mostly on foot or bike. Unless accustomed to biking in heavy traffic of hundreds of bicyclists, visitors should walk, rickshaw or taxi. The most populous bike-riding area in the world, with strict paths and rules to guide the contingencies of moving bicyclists. Watching the bicyclists is part of the experience. This form of transport works well for Beijing, a city with a growing population and smog problems. Opt for van or taxi or sedans with A/C. Buses are crowed and language stressful.

PEDESTRIAN-FRIENDLY
6 on a scale of 1-10
A CHALLENGE

Pedestrian-friendly in and around tourist and main business centers. Off the main wide streets are smaller narrow streets much like Manhattan, shared by a moving population and delivery trucks. Moving to another section of the city by rickshaw or on foot is difficult. Traffic is heavy and walking becomes risky. Anything with wheels has the right-of-way. Guided tours, walking tours and guides are recommended for short visits to get the most from your trip. There's much to see and do.

MONEY
RENMINBI (RMB)
A CHALLENGE

The "peoples currency" is an official term for Chinese currency. FEC (foreign currency certificates) are issued for visitors. These are more easily exchanged and can be exchanged upon departure. The local currency is handy for markets and daily use, but can't be exchanged. At most tourist areas there is a price for foreign visitors and one for locals. Use the concierge and banks for exchange; ATMs are becoming more popular. Travelers' checks are wise. Prices vary and tips are not usually appropriate. Ask or consult a hospitality or travel professional. Generally---a visit here is very expensive.

Destination Realities   "Best Practice" Travel Advice

POLLUTION REALITY
4 on a scale of 1-10
DODGY

Growth in industry and car congestion has boosted this city into a dangerous smog zone. Dust from new construction colors your impression of the city, big and polluted. The city is spread out, which helps. On hot and muggy days, take a handkerchief to breathe through, especially if you're out in a pedicab or rickshaw. The bikes with their separate lane and transport infrastructure have helped address this problem, a positive solution for such a populous city center.

LANGUAGE
Chinese - Mandarin
A CHALLENGE

Standard Chinese is based on Mandarin. It is spoken by about 70% of the population. Cantonese and several other languages and hundreds of dialects make up official and secondary languages. English, though not widely spoken, is used by the younger generation, those in the hospitality and business sectors. Communication may be a frustrating factor in your experience. Learning a few words is always suggested, hiring a guide and /or translator is recommended. Guide books and a phrase book help. Read the local English papers.

POLITICAL REALITY
Socialist state
A CHALLENGE

Capital: Beijing
Largest City: Shanghai

China boasts the world's oldest continuous civilization. The Communist Party took control in 1949. Recent efforts by a younger generation show increasingly popular demand for democratic reforms. A single-party state, where the Communist Party controls most aspects of daily life through mass membership organizations and professional associations, has been evolving since the 1970s. China is witnessing a movement toward a more market-driven economy but political transition has been slow and controlling.

ECONOMIC REALITY
5 on a scale of 1-10
A CHALLENGE

China is expected to become the world's largest economy and is seeking to join the World Trade Organization. While most of the economy is controlled by the state, new market challenges have been introduced, and in a selective way, accepted. Massive education and reform for the rural population are major challenges for the 21st century. Cultural unity and protection for the individual and group are an underlying force that is challenged by a controlled economy and a socialist state political system.

AIRPORT FACILITIES
Airport Code: PEK
City Code: PEK
CAUTION

Other Airports:
Shanghai
Hong Kong
and many others

☛ URBAN CTR
18 miles
30 - 60 minutes
$20.00 - 45.00 USD
usually prearranged

☛ ✈ ALLOW
2 hrs. check-in
1-2 hrs. transport

Beijing Capital Airport. One of the main airports for International flights. Overcrowded for the current infrastructure. Terminal One is under construction. Expect delays and unplanned congestion coming and going. Limited business facilities. A tour desk and a medical center are available. No current airport Website available. Airport improvements and competition between airports are on the rise. Contact: 10-645-642-47.

BE POLITE: *Listen and observe.*

HAVE MANNERS: *Dress and behave as others around you.*

SHOW INTEREST: *Leave your ego behind, ask questions diplomatically.*

MAKE AN EFFORT: *Fit in. Interact. Engage.*

BE POLITE

Protocol and respect for elders are highly regarded in this society. The family, school, work and local community are the personal safe havens where a collective consciousness governs the group. The head of the group takes responsibilities and other individuals follow. Western influences and pockets of Western business practice are making their way into the business culture, but a collective consciousness is a stable basis for thought and practice. Respecting what someone else respects is polite. Critical judgment clouds polite social interaction. A nod or short bow is a polite greeting gesture. Handshakes are also acceptable, but wait for the host to extend his or her hand first.

HAVE MANNERS

The virtues of kindness, proprietary righteousness, and faithfulness are pervasive within the families and collective groups. Outsiders are not considered to value these virtues in the same way, so there is hesitancy, distrust and dislike of outsiders. Don't take it personally and respect their perspective. Your mannerisms can be considered arrogant or rude in this society, which is very correct, proper and protocol-sensitive. Before leaving on your trip, it is wise to consult a cultural specialist to prepare for important business and social meetings. Keep gestures to a minimum. Take note and inquire, colors are important and represent specific occasions.

SHOW INTEREST

Showing interest is reflected by your understanding of and conformity to general protocols. There's much suffering and poverty in China, but the people are proud of their civilization and the many inventions and discoveries that originated there. Show interest in family life, arts, history and new economy issues.

MAKE AN EFFORT

To communicate, use short English sentences with clear diction. Don't use sports and war analogies or trendy jargon. They want to learn and speak English to communicate. Make an effort to be punctual. Learn something new.

10 Highly Effective Words to "Get By"

1. **A Greeting**	ni-HAo	ni hao
2. **Please**	chin	qi'ng
3. **Thank You**	shieh shieh	xi_e xi_e
4. **Yes**	shy-e	shi
5. **No**	bu shye	bu shi
6. **Toilet**	SHEE sho dyen	ki sho dyen
7. **How Much**	djua ju-o sha ao tchien	zhe duo_shao qian
8. **Help**	bang/man	bang man
9. **Excuse Me**	CHIN ri ahg	qi ng ra ng
10. **Police**	DJING cha ju	jing cha ju

Great Connections & Community

Jot down important phone numbers, contacts, addresses. Great shops and restaurants---get their Email and Web address. **SCRIBBLE NOTES** and info before, during and after!

Airport & Airline Update

Beijing Int'l Airport　　　　**http://210.75.250.252/eversion**
A complex transition from government oversight to private groups and contracts limits online information. Only very general information available. No recent updates.

Air China　　　　**www.airchina.com**
China Airlines　　　　**www.china-airlines.com**
China Southern Airlines　　　　**www.cs-air.com/en**
Cathay Pacific Airways　　　　**www.cathaypacific.com**

A variety of general airline information.

CNTO-China National Tourist Office　　　　**www.cnto.org**
A general information site with official tourism travel updates and vistor information and history. Contacts available by email directly.

Moving Forward Advisory: Beijing airport is run efficiently, but it is slow-moving yet progressive on infrastructure improvements to keep pace with demands in growth and usage. Budget 2 hours for domestic and 3 hours for international check-in from time of scheduled departure. Ask advice of airline or agency for current expectations of procedures. Patience.

TEAR out & TAKE

95

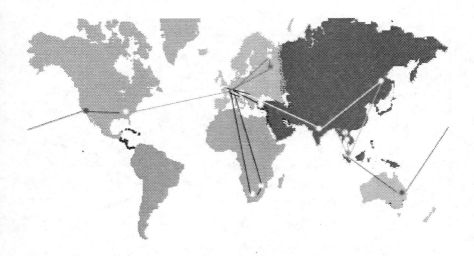

TEAR out & TAKE

| GREAT |
| GOOD |
| A CHALLENGE |
| DODGY |
| CAUTION |

Traveling by train is a great way to get around. Earplugs come in handy to muffle noises of all sorts.

Personal Space
DODGY

Toilets
A CHALLENGE

Cleanliness & Bugs
DODGY

PEOPLE SPACE & PERSPIRATION

Many people live and work in very small living quarters. Space, luxury items and Western amenities are available on a limited and restricted basis. A nation of very industrious people. In collective groups you get used to each other and get along on some level. Different hygiene rituals vary. New foods and smells are very different and may be offensive. Expect your senses or "comfort zone" to be challenged.

TOILETS & TRIBULATIONS

Expect Western-style toilets in Western or Western conscientious establishments. Prepare for squat Asian-style toilets with minimum amenities. Cleanliness is more important in the home and community than in public areas. Facilities tend to be rare or non-existent in noodle-lined stall and market areas. E&DS (Eating and Drinking Strategically) is suggested to limit unpleasant toilet experiences. Most tourist attractions have facilities, but maintenance is often a problem.

HYGIENE & HIGH JINKS

A densely populated city with old and new construction gives the appearance of dusty but clean. Older buildings and accommodations are a bit run down. Cigarette burns here and there make things look shabbier or less clean than they actually are. The Chinese are heavy smokers and the residual effects are around. This city has many upmarket hotels, limited middle market and its share of sleazy accommodations.

Health risks include diarrhea caused by contaminated fruits, vegetables and water. Drink bottled water and use it for all washing rituals as a precaution.

BUGS:

A big city offers bugs in a variety of ways. Watch your accommodations and what and where you eat. I had bug fears and concerns as in any other big city.

Western Style

and everything
inbetween

Asian Style

Toilet
Stories...

CHINA

Control and rules apply to all citizens and so too, to a
certain extent, for visitors. My memory of the train toilet is
its cleanliness diminishing with time. I was on the train for
24 hours. There were 2 toilets for women---one Asian and
one Western. Both were bare of anything but porcelain.
You go in, hold your nose and quickly leave. Toilet paper
is your option. I developed a tolerance for train toilets
because the train ride is usually an opportunity to see
much countryside and many rural towns not easily visited
any other way.

Singapore

Singapore
Singapore & Environs

A city of festivals, luxury shops, hawker stalls and stinky Durian. Views from the public buses in and out of town impress the senses with a tidy, bustling, multicultural city. Feng Shui and people busy with affairs of a personal and professional nature. A world import/export hub where land is built-out to reach new ships. Humidity to humble your pace. Sticky but cool A/C. Black pepper crab, noodles and satay.

DISCOVERIES

■ *Singapore is wired. Cyberheart Online is a delightful cybercafe find on Orchard Road with Net-stations ready for action. An Emailer's delight. Broadband is everywhere!*
■ *Huge cranes and massive ships move world cargo from the hemispheres, a pit stop to load and unload wares from everywhere.*
■ *Tipping is not necessary.*
■ *Public transportation is the best mode of getting around. To keep car traffic contained only the rich can afford to pay the "fee" to drive a personal vehicle in the city.*
■ *Hawker stalls are a culinary treat with* every assortment of Asian and Continental cuisine. Not fast food as much as it is fast fixed food, served hot and fresh.
■ *Indeed, you can be fined or worse if you do not observe and obey local laws and public rules. Singapore and Zurich have much in common---strict rules and regulations or else; you will be punished.*
■ *Only hail cabs in areas where there are no double yellow lines or there is no taxi queue.*
■ *Air conditioning is just about everywhere.*
■ *Everything is very expensive - don't eat Mexican.*

MAGICAL MOMENTS

■ *Discovering Singapore through the experiences of hospitable friends, **Nat and Stacie**.*
■ *The Chinese and Indian "10 Words to Get By" came in handy to communicate.*
■ *Sweating through one of the most messy and delightful meals on the Boat Quay overlooking the bay. Black pepper crab, and a table full of food to feast in, on,* around and through. Towel and sink usage complimentary on exit.
■ *Toasting travels, travel dreams, travel stories and a meeting of new friends.*
■ *Working through, '"should we stay or should we go" to Cambodia. The U.S. signed a most-favored-nation trading agreement. Heard it on the news.*

Destination Realities

"Best Practice" Travel Advice

POPULATION
3.5 million
GREAT

This small main island is surrounded by 50 islets. It possesses a rich multiracial heritage and a strong tourism and trade reputation and caters to an influx of 7-8 million visitors a year. Known as one of the busiest port cities, Singapore is a key harbor and holds free-trade status with world trade and cargo reflecting the diverse mix of the local population. Congenial, modern and open to visitors from all walks of life. Very comfortable and easy to get to know in 2 to 3 days. A professional's city.

WEATHER
tropical all year, humid
A CHALLENGE

About 80 miles from the equator, humidity of the tropics rules and it rains, more frequently in the months of November to January. This city has made efforts to try and tame mother nature much like in the southern U.S.A. Air conditioning is installed in most public and private places. Weather here is consistent in its humidity and wet nature...you WILL wither and not wear it well, especially at first. Be advised, adapt to a more casual and "au naturale" style. Getting caught in the rain and bad hair don't generally hinder first impressions.

TRANSPORT
1-public transport, 2-walk
GREAT

Malay:
Airport -lapangan terbang
Train - keretapi
Bus - bas
Subway - (MRT) airtee
Taxi - taksi
Where is - di manakah

All forms of transportation for all preferred styles of transport are available. Air-conditioned taxis are expensive but available 24 hours. The MRT-Mass Rapid Rail is a reliable, clean and inexpensive transport mode to get around. Public buses are easy to use, though it takes more time for scheduled stops. To and from the airport you can take the MRT and a bus mix. Be careful to hail taxis only in double-yellow-lined areas or where there is no taxi queue in sight. The car steering wheel is located on the right while driving is on the left.

PEDESTRIAN-FRIENDLY
9 on a scale of 1-10
GREAT

As a world shopping center, the city has many areas that are both pedestrian and shopping-friendly. A combination of great public transportation and a compact centralized cityscape with easily accessible suburbs makes this city one of the most "pedestrian-friendly." Cars are very expensive to own and this lessens the world urban trend to cram as many cars into a city as possible. Streets and public transportation are clean and visitor-friendly offering a great experience no matter what the reason for the visit, business or pleasure.

MONEY
Singapore Dollar (SGD)
A CHALLENGE

Singapore is a city and a country positioned to handle all kinds of transactions as a gateway to Southeast Asia. The banking and trading systems are well-established. The cost of living is high for this tropical city. Fees and regulations for imported goods to outrageous taxes on cars, a policy to curb pollution, translates into expensive. Some good bargains can be had on art pieces, electronics and various other goods outside the city. Prices generally are high, credit cards are accepted and ATMs are readily available.

POLLUTION REALITY
6 on a scale of 1-10
A CHALLENGE

Singapore and Rio are both able to boast a tropical rain forest within their limits. Unfortunately they are both challenged with "urban progress" in nearby areas that contributes to dense levels of pollution. A tropical humidity can exacerbate respiratory and pollution-prone sensitivities. Smoke from burning forests sometimes hovers over the city. Port cities are also heavy with trucks and boats and they contribute to air and noise pollution. Any port city is challenged with pollution, so is Singapore.

LANGUAGE
English and local (Malay)
GREAT

Singapore is a multiethnic society which tries to balance diversity and the cooperation of the Singaporean citizenship. Three main language groups are encouraged on a national scale: Chinese (Mandarin), Malay and Indian (Tamil). English, a widely spoken language, is the language of business, administration, education and international commerce. It is widely understood, especially by the younger generations and international professionals living in and passing through Singapore.

POLITICAL REALITY
Republic of Singapore
GOOD

Capital: Singapore

A parliamentary system with strong influence has been established and put in place by the People's Action Party and a long-reigning prime minister. Challenges are for a new generation of decision makers to be included in government decisions and policy. Diverse but small parties desire a more influential say in political and economic decision making. Challenges are for current leadership to pass on power to new leadership. Managing growth and stability in a growing economic region is a political challenge today.

ECONOMIC REALITY
8 on a scale of 1-10
GOOD

Singapore is a power port and power player in regional and world trade. Major stabilizing forces have been put in place through progressive policy to unite and structure a developed Singapore. Traditional export products and services include petroleum refining, machinery and shipbuilding. High-growth leaders are electronics, technology, finance and banking services. Singapore is a wired city and leads with benchmark techniques to process its trade and investments. Limited physical land leads to high cost of living.

AIRPORT FACILITIES
Airport Code: SIN
City Code: SIN
GREAT

Southeast Asia Hub Airport

☛ **URBAN CTR**
10 miles
20-40 minutes
$25.00 USD
☛ ✈ **ALLOW**
1.5 hrs. check-in
2 hrs. transport

Changi International Airport, Singapore. One of the most spectacular airports in the world. A mini-city with amenities to suit every need. If you need some electronics or gadgets you can get them here. One of the first "Net-ready" airports, Changi airport offers the global-mobile a cybercenter and a transit hotel right in the airport. 4-hour layover---take free city tour. Check **www.changi.airport.com.sg** or (65)541-9828.

BE POLITE: *Listen and observe.*

HAVE MANNERS: *Dress and behave as others around you.*

SHOW INTEREST: *Leave your ego behind, ask questions diplomatically.*

MAKE AN EFFORT: *Fit in. Interact. Engage.*

BE POLITE

"Singaporean" manners and etiquette vary by ethnicities. Chinese is the largest ethnic population making up the "Singaporean nationality," with Malay and Indian to follow. A general attention to Asian customs and, on your part, a restrained approach of Western casual mannerisms may serve you well. A handshake is an acceptable greeting gesture of introduction for men and only to women if a woman extends her hand first. Otherwise, a humble, slight bow of the head and smile will cover the bases.

HAVE MANNERS

Respect for elders and senior-level professionals takes precedence in general exchanges, social and business. Touching someone who is not family or very familiar is restricted and formal. Asian influences and characteristics of intercultural exchanges include "saving face," and different interpretations of the nodding of the head. A nod of yes to a Westerner generally means one is listening and acknowledging your communications, it doesn't necessarily mean agreement. Observe and mimic formality and tradition. Don't hesitate to ask a hotel concierge or local travel professional for some etiquette tips.

SHOW INTEREST

Singaporeans are proud of their nation and its position and power as a finance, trade and industrial crossroads for Asia. Technology and telecommunications are key topics to take interest in and ask about. Popular media and a trendy young generation of professionals are eager to introduce Singapore.

MAKE AN EFFORT

Singapore is bustling with Western influences and internationalism, but the underlying social fabric is a mixture of Asian cultures. Make an effort to asses the individual and engage appropriately. You will easily feel welcomed.

10 Highly Effective Words to "Get By"

Malay

1. **A Greeting**	heh-LOW	hehlow
2. **Please**	TAW-long	tolong
3. **Thank You**	tay-REE-ma ka-SEEH	terima kassih
4. **Yes**	i-AH	ya
5. **No**	TEE-dak	ti-dak
6. **Toilet**	Tahn-DAH	tandas
7. **How Much**	BEH-ra pa-KAH HAR-ga eNE	berapakar harga ini
8. **Help**	MEH-noh -long	menolong; tolong
9. **Excuse Me**	min-TAAH ma-AAF	minta maaf
10. **Police**	paw-LEE	Polis

Great Connections & Community

Jot down important phone numbers/contacts/addresses. Great shops and restaurants---get their Email and Web address. **SCRIBBLE NOTES** and info before, during and after!

Airport & Airline Update

Singapore Int'l Airport   **www.changi.airport.co.sg**
A comprehesive and content-rich airport site. Passenger advisories not mentioned, but prompt feedback results with email inquiries. Look for news flash updates on homepage.

Singapore Airlines   **www.singaporeair.com**
A comprehensive, information and service-oriented site. News updates are current and media advisories are revealed on homepage in a timely manner.

Singapore Tourism Board   **www.singapore-usa.com**
An easy-to-follow, comprehensive information-rich site, especially for tips and culture. Offers access to contacts and further information.

Moving Forward Advisory: Singapore, a major Asian hub, is prompt with its attention to current FAA recommendations and action. Anticipate and budget more time for check-in procedures. Contact your airline for expected delays or schedule reductions or changes due to international flight rerouting and adjustments.

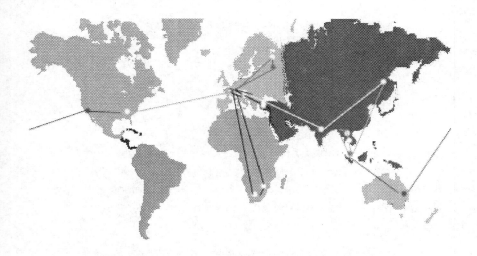

GREAT
GOOD
A CHALLENGE
DODGY
CAUTION

Personal Space
GREAT

Toilets
GOOD

Cleanliness & Bugs
GOOD

PUBLIC SPACE & PERSPIRATION

Singapore is becoming more populous, but more importantly it is becoming crowded with visitors from all walks of life. Each carries his or her own social and cultural lifestyle. Beware of local rules: no smoking, no jaywalking and no spitting are allowed without serious penalty, even for visitors. Jail time is enforced for offenses that may only be a petty crime or unobserved broken laws in your hometown. Find a taxi queue when hailing taxis, check rules or ask for assistance when unsure. Social interaction is to keep your distance. Don't display affection or make disturbances or loud conversation in public. A bubble of distance is appropriate.

Follow the local rules and regulations. Pay attention.

TOILETS & TRIBULATIONS

The government subsidizes many services and is able to control higher standards and offerings to a visiting public. Public toilets are generally spotless and many are pay-as-you-go setups. Others in off-the-beaten-path or outside of general public places and markets may be quite the opposite of what you are used to. Asian squat toilets exist but have generally been replaced by Western-style toilets.

HYGIENE & HIGH JINKS

Singapore is like the Zurich of Asia: strict adherence to government regulations and enforced policy and rules are in place to maintain a clean and tidy city. Because of this the city is known as one of the cleanest cities.

Drinking water is safe. Hawker stalls are regulated with strict sanitary regulations that must be adhered to.

BUGS:

It's a tropical climate and bugs exist though the city authorities have done a great job creating concrete mass housing, shopping and business areas with major insect-resistance techniques ---heavy concrete and air conditioning. Cracks and spaces between doors and windows in more open-style housing and accommodations allow crawling creatures in. Geckos are common, harmless visitors. Most establishments for visitors are sealed to retain air conditioning and heating efficiencies.

Western Style

Asian Style

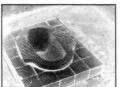

and everything
i n b e t w e e n

Toilet
Stories...

SINGAPORE

Finding public "facilities" is generally easy. Singapore prides itself on cleanliness and a tourist's high standards. So toilets abound. I didn't encounter any pay toilets, but it wouldn't surprise me if they had them. Singapore is known for all kinds of laws and fines for "public properness." There is rumor, however, that there is a "no flush" fine. Expect most toilets in higher-standard establishments to be clean. However, any urban area with heavy traffic makes for messy toilets here and there, no matter where you are. And it is likely you will encounter an Asian-style toilet during your visit unless you are travelling 5-star all the way. Have toilet paper, will travel.

Cambodia

Cambodia
Siem Reap & Environs

A provincial capital. Siem Reap's colonial remnants and open housing on stilts strikes a Westerner's remembrance of the movie Killing Fields. Mustering up tolerance to embrace the tropical climate. Courage to follow armed guides to sites of Khmer bas-relief stories of unfathomable conquests and power. Tree roots pushed through earth to clutch and eat ancient broken buildings. Glowing geckos.

DISCOVERIES

■ *The U.S. granted Cambodia most-favored-nation status in 1996.*

■ *There are windows of opportunity to travel to Cambodia. It is periodically on a State Department list of countries to avoid. Check travel.state.gov.*

■ *Underdevelopment is quickly changing to development. Siem Reap is growing for the tourist dollar at a yet-to-be-known expense.*

■ *Bas-relief walls for miles in the Angkor Complex of Khmer-era ruins belittle mere visitors to insignificant gnats.*

■ *Archaeological wonders of power, culture, art and beauty are revealed in crumbled ruins and rebuilt temple complexes guided by rifle-armed soldiers, now state tour guides.   Don't go off the beaten path without a guide; caution---land mines.*

■ *802 A.D. - most cited date being the "Age of Angkor," Southeast Asia's greatest civilization and time.*

■ *Guides and transport clamor at the departure doors of the airport. Be prepared to make choices. It pays to know where you're going in advance, or advise transport-clamoring touts you are taken care of, if indeed you are.*

■ *Entry to ruins is at least $20.00 a day.*

MAGICAL MOMENTS

■ *Entering Angkor Wat's main temple complex just before sunset, imagining the powerful kings who ruled. A rainbow appeared.*

■ *Squatting on a smooth stone carved hall doorway watching pink streaks of sky fade into darkness.*

■ *Peeking over the edge of the rooftop of our colonial-style accommodations, taking in a sweeping dance step or two before walking the main street to grab a bite to eat.*

■ *Making young girls laugh and giggle when I was singing '"no, no, no thank you" in Khmer to sooth my anxious feelings of these always-offering-something children.*

Destination Realities

"Best Practice" Travel Advice

POPULATION
Under 20,000
GOOD

The former Khmer Kingdom included parts of Thailand, Laos and Vietnam. Today the country's population is approximately 10-11 million. Phnom Penh is the capital and commercial center with a growing urban population, about 1 million. Siem Reap is a principle former colonial town. Currently it is a provincial capital with a local population servicing the new tourism, historical and archaeological interests. Siem Reap is the town supporting visitors to the ruins. Easy-to-know town in 1 day. Visiting achaeological sites, 2 to 5 days.

WEATHER
tropical, slight seasons
A CHALLENGE

A tropical monsoon climate to adjust to. May to November expect 1 to 3 hours of rain or slight showers in the afternoon. November to May is the best season to travel, dry season. Casual attire, very casual, fits this climate best. Be prepared for rain and showers. Do as the locals do, find cover or endure a light sprinkle---you'll dry off. Land of paddies and forests dominated by the Mekong River and Tonle Sap.

TRANSPORT
1st walk, 2nd taxi-car
GOOD

Khmer:
Airport - yeal youn huas
Train - rout phleoung
Bus - lan thom monous
Taxi - tukse
Where is - nouv eir na

Getting to Siem Reap is getting easier, particularly by air. "Open Sky" agreements have recently been put in place, major airlines now fly directly in or through Phnom Penh. Overland there are several routes recommended by travel agents and guide books. Roads are in disrepair, border crossings precarious and banditry is still high. Siem Reap is a small town with attention to serving tourists. Hired cars are recommended as guides to ruins, now a World Heritage Site. Walking the town is also very doable.

PEDESTRIAN FRIENDLY
7 on a scale of 1-10
A CHALLENGE

Siem Reap, close to the Angkor Complex, is about 7 miles from the closest temple. Walking in and about the town can be unexpectedly wet and muddy. The entire town center hasn't been paved over with cement everywhere. Transport to the ruins is readily available. Walking through the crumbling ruins is safe, demands attention and a bit of endurance. There are long walks between buildings in open, hot space. The tourism authority is supporting the local community to develop a visitor and pedestrian-friendly center.

MONEY
Cambodian RIEL (KHR)
GOOD

This is a poor nation and one recovering from political and economic unrest. Tourism is a relatively new industry and prices vary with services and standards. Both U.S. dollars and RIELs can be used. Exchange is easily available at banks and money changers. Credit cards are only accepted at the few upscale hotels and merchants able to afford it for the influx of card-totting visitors. Carry small amounts of cash and change for each day. Travellers' checks are not readily exchanged or accepted.

POLLUTION REALITY
6 on a scale of 1-10
DODGY

How this provincial town hits you in this respect is relative to where you come from and how you view "pollution." For the local community this area was a quiet, agriculturally structured village. Then it was influenced by foreigners and French colonial structures of Western design. Infrastructure in sewage and water initiatives were limited. Water safety is a concern; take precautions. Cars and gas-dependent mopeds are on the rise causing, concern. The influx of aircraft and visitors is causing more pollution issues.

LANGUAGE
Khmer, French, English
GOOD

A majority of the population speaks Khmer. An older generation speaks French and the younger generation is picking up English, particularly to service foreigners and the tourist dollar. "Pop" or popular English is much of what you will hear and be communicating with. English is learned by watching television and reading magazines. Trading partners who have a large influence find a language in common to communicate, generally French, English and some Asian languages.

POLITICAL REALITY
Transition Democracy
A CHALLENGE

Capital: Phnom Penh

Political and economic stability are a delicate balance and challenge. Granted most-favored-nation status in 1996, the Kingdom of Cambodia has struggled. 1998 brought in some stability with national elections and a new coalition government gaining recognition. Contentions and distrust are residual concerns of local party members. Be cautious and stay clear of local group gatherings or demonstrations. Adhere to government advisories. Downplay your wealth; banditry for cash has been a longtime part of lifestyle for some.

ECONOMIC REALITY
5 on a scale of 1-10
DODGY

Currently Cambodia is economically on the rise. However, Cambodia has been hit recently by the Asian economic crisis, civil violence, political infighting and flight of foreign investment and tourism. The population lacks education and productive skills. The current political stability has the government and foreign investors forging multilateral relationships to address these concerns. This economy offers natural resources and historical treasures.

AIRPORT FACILITIES
Airport Code: REP
City Code: REP

Other Airports:
Phnom Penh
(Main Country Airport)

☛ **URBAN CTR**
5 miles
5-15 minutes
$3 - 10. USD

☛ ✈ **ALLOW**
1 hr. check-in
30 min. transport

Siem Reap International airport is small (walk outside from building to plane) and has been taking on increased loads of visitors. Siem Reap and direct flights bypassing Phnom Penh started in 1996. A recent news report refers to renovations in the works. Capacity was 200 passengers. Limited on amenities, the airport is under review for major renovation and/or a new airport site location. Construction may be in progress.

BE POLITE: *Listen and observe.*

HAVE MANNERS: *Dress and behave as others around you.*

SHOW INTEREST: *Leave your ego behind, ask questions diplomatically.*

MAKE AN EFFORT: *Fit in. Interact. Engage.*

BE POLITE

General politeness is ingrained in this culture. Historically it is a kingdom with vast lands and wealth. A respectful greeting in a slight bow with hands clasped lightly together and the greeting *johm riab sua* should be practiced and used as an initial greeting. Eye contact is generally averted unless you are in areas and situations where there is a mix of international visitors.

HAVE MANNERS

Keep hand gestures to a minimum and respect social distance customs. Don't pat anyone on the head, even young children. This is considered the most important part of the body in spiritual customs and tradition. The feet are the least important and not to be walked over or pointed with. Casual Western sitting positions with legs crossed and the sole of the shoe across one knee are considered extremely rude and disrespectful. Keep soles of feet on the ground.

SHOW INTEREST

The Cambodian culture and former kingdom are strong traditions with which Cambodians identify. Generations of communist rule and the execution and flight of the educated classes have left Cambodian citizens struggling. Be respectful and interested on any level with all Cambodians.

MAKE AN EFFORT

Multilateral agreements to create new economic stability in Cambodia have been ongoing. Efforts to "tourismize" the historical ruins and ancient sites have mixed reviews with locals. Some see it as an opportunity, others see it as commercialism and a Western invasion. Be understanding and tolerant of these views and make an effort to learn about the culture and the proud people of Cambodia. Their traditions and culture have been around for centuries.

10 Highly Effective Words to "Get By"

1. A Greeting	jOOhm-ree-up sOO-ah	johm riab sua
2. Please	sohm	suom
3. Thank You	or-gOOn	arkun
4. Yes	baat (male) jaas female)	bat (male) jas (female)
5. No	(o)d-tayh	dte
6. Toilet	bong-gOO-un	bawngkohn
7. How Much	bohn-mAAn	ponh maan
8. Help	jOOm-noo-ay	juay kh'nyohm
9. Excuse Me	sOOm dtoah	suom tous
10. Police	dtom-roo-ut	tomroot

Great Connections & Community

Jot down important phone numbers, contacts, addresses. Great shops and restaurants---get their Email and Web Address.
SCRIBBLE NOTES and info before, during and after!

Airport & Airline Update

Siem Reap Int'l Airport   **No site available**
Economic instability persists in this country. Any airport information or ongoing development plans remain extremely limited at this time.

Royal Air Cambodge   **www.royal-air-cambodge.com**
The site is not in service at this time.

Royal Cambodian Embassy   **www.embassy.org/cambodia**
An official government site sponsored by the Embassy of Cambodia in Washington, D.C. General information and direct embassy staff contact is available via email or phone. No current updates. This is one of the main resources available for Cambodia online and off.

Moving Forward Advisory: Caution, information research and planning are critical for travel to Cambodia. Considerable economic instability has this country, its airports in Phnom Penh and Siem Reap and its national and local airlines struggling with upkeep and management. Check with agencies specializing in Asia for current advisories for entry and visits to Cambodia at this time.

TEAR OUT & TAKE

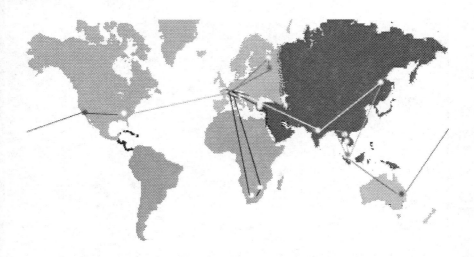

DARE to Travel the World

> *GREAT*
> *GOOD*
> *A CHALLENGE*
> *DODGY*
> *CAUTION*

Personal Space
A CHALLENGE

PEOPLE SPACE & PERSPIRATION

Cambodians tend to live in nuclear families, instead of extended families. However, living conditions have changed dramatically, differing in urban and rural areas. Extended and nuclear families are generally close in relationships and close in living space. Social customs and tradition within families and friends provide a comfort zone of closeness and camaraderie. Westerners are not allowed in this space and it is disrespectful to be "chummy" unless you have been invited to do so. Traditional living style is with open walls and no doors, tropical living. Urban centers are a mix of old, new, traditional, colonial and everything in between.

Toilets
GOOD

TOILETS & TRIBULATIONS

Asian-style toilets are traditional and are found as an option in most public toilets which are few and far between, depending on where you are. Western toilets are found with Western establishments catering to Internationals. Expect toilet challenges anywhere you are. If and when you make it to Cambodia, you will know to be tolerant.

Cleanliness & Bugs
A CHALLENGE

HYGIENE & HIGH JINKS

Renovated guesthouses and Western-style accommodations (with air conditioning) offer the closest comforts of hygiene and bug-free environments. However, tropical climates, however tamed or cemented over, can't stop mother nature. Cambodians respect nature and its creatures.

Clean, drinkable water is an issue for locals and visitors alike. Be cautious and drink, wash face and brush teeth with a good brand of bottled water.

BUGS:

Beware of bugs, spiders and friendly glowing geckos.

Western Style

and everything
inbetween

Asian Style

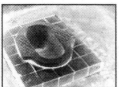

Toilet Stories...

CAMBODIA

A tiled, mini, Western-styled bathroom, in a newly
renovated guesthouse accommodation, left me with
no nightmares, toilet trauma or horror stories. By this
time, my toilet tolerance had reached a high level
of "lighten up and you'll live through it." A band of
geckos did troll the walls at night. I imagined they
were capturing crawling creatures, thus allowing me
to rest. The sparse room, with eye-distracting green
mosquito-netted single iron beds, was a deal at
$27.00 U.S. a night. Geckos and all.

Thailand

Thailand
Bangkok & Environs

MEMORIES

A flashy airport with a great tourism office, and a memorable jump from air-conditioned international airport to humid, wet, tropical big-city trains, buses and bustling life. Golden-sashed Buddhas, glitter, flower markets and SUDA's restaurant offering Pad Thai, coconut ice cream and shelter from the city afternoon rains. Gems, discretionary gem sellers, 5-star hotels, river boats and barbecued squid on a stick.

DISCOVERIES

■ The desire to shop is increased by a desire to escape the city heat, humidity and intermittent rains. Much daily sweating.

■ Well-intentioned, English-speaking, Western-clad Thais may assist you with directions and steer you to the "final day of gem bargains...close out today" for their commission.

■ Street vendors with the most entertaining-looking foods display their foodware. Food's a great bargain. Fresh pineapple, banana fritters and squid on a stick are to salivate for. Try them.

■ Eating from street vendors was cheap and good. Mind the occasional ants feasting about also. Great street noodles.

■ Electricity comes and goes, so be prepared for some short, dark moments.

■ Public transportation is easy and cheap. The city boat shuttle is a treat for viewing the city, buildings, and areas. A great way to get around.

■ Internet access is to be found if you look for it.

■ Reclining Buddhas of great stature abound draped in gold cloth. Incense and offerings to the gods prevail.

MAGICAL MOMENTS

■ Stopping on a main street in Bangkok to pick up a quick bite of roasted squid on a stick and get directions from a local.

■ Arriving at Hau Hin, a Thai resort town about 3-hours south of Bangkok. Feasting and walking all day. Fishing villages, small islands and a boat ride to island caves and a local rainforest area.

■ Jumping off a tuk-tuk transport vehicle on the island of Ko Samui to find Internet access, the Sandy Resort, new friends, including **Gail**, to dine with at the Pink Panther Restaurant---BoPhut Beach.

■ A tropical mix of big city, resorts and easy living with a calm breeze keeps memories of Thailand floating in and out.

Destination Realities

"Best Practice" Travel Advice

POPULATION
9 million
A CHALLENGE

The city boasts a modern urban center with the eccentricities and confusion of a huge Western metropolis. Mix in heat, sweat and the Thais traditions, rituals and commerce, and you have a world city and major trading and commercial center of Asia. Tourism is a major economic sector so you will find plenty of top tourism resources, cultural and commercial venues to cater to your needs across all economic levels. English is widely spoken in general. Takes 3 to 4 days to get to know. World class.

WEATHER
tropical year-around
A CHALLENGE

Bangkok weather remains consistent with humid city temperatures much of the year, peaking in the 90s Fahrenheit and cooling off to the 60s other months. Monsoon in October usually means flooding in many areas of Thailand with regular showers. This doesn't slow down the pace of city business or progress. Take an umbrella and be prepared to keep going or take a break in moments of heavy rain. More casual clothing with an unpressed look is the norm. Light, drip-dry apparel suggested.

TRANSPORT
1st walk, 2nd taxi/bus
A CHALLENGE

Airport - sa narm bin
Train - rod fai
Bus - rod mai
Subway - rod fai tai din
Taxi - rod thaek sii
Where is - you tee nai

Popular transport includes buses from the airport to 3 city centers. Taxis from one location to another are suggested. A variety of trains, buses and river shuttle boats form a network of connections in the city, rural and resort areas. Tuk-tuks offer little protection from pollution and the elements. Motorcycle taxis are available to cut through stop-dead traffic but are risky. Walking, bus, taxi or boat hopping are best practices, convenient and cost-effective. Cars drive on the left and traffic is unpredictable and congested.

PEDESTRIAN-FRIENDLY
6 on a scale of 1-10
A CHALLENGE

Walking is a main mode of transportation. Biking is usual in many areas outside the city. With the population growth, space in the city has become dense and congested; pedestrian traffic has increased. Narrow streets and crowded market aisles make walking leisurely sometimes difficult. Be aware of your surroundings and keep a map with you to help others help you when you need directions or get lost. Thai people are kind and helping. Sometimes they may be smiling and embarrassed because they are unable to assist.

MONEY
BAHT (BHT)
GOOD

A world center for commerce and tourism, Bangkok offers many opportunities to exchange money. The exchange may vary daily so unless you are exchanging vast quantities and prefer to carry cash (not recommended for tourists and short-term visitors), use credit cards, ATMs and bank exchange services. Economic stability offers good value on products, services and entertainment. Be cautious about authenticity and quality.

GREAT
GOOD
A CHALLENGE
DODGY
CAUTION

POLLUTION REALITY
6 on a scale of 1-10
A CHALLENGE

Tropical weather, traffic congestion and a shifting population into the city attract a growing share of pollutants and industry. Rainy season, while it washes away much, leaves the air stagnant and humid and city air pollution lingers. Take refuge often in air-conditioned environments (there are plenty) and don't let a bit of smog and humidity slow you down.

LANGUAGE
Thai
A CHALLENGE

With linguistic threads from official Chinese, Thai is the distinct national language, tough for visitors and not even that easy for Thais themselves. English is an unofficial language of business and hospitality to accommodate the millions of multinational visitors doing business and/or visiting Thailand. Other languages include Chinese (Mandarin), Lao, Khmer and Malay. Check with local resources or contacts on proper name addressing conventions. Note nicknames and first names as accepted way to address each other.

POLITICAL REALITY
Constitutional Monarchy
GOOD

Capital: Bangkok
Former Capital: Ayutthaya

Referred to as the Kingdom of Thailand, since WWII the balance of power has been split between the military and civilian leaders. The word Thai means "free." The Thai are proud of never being colonized. The constitutional monarchy enjoys strong global relations and trade and is working to stabilize the country.

ECONOMIC REALITY
7 on a scale of 1-10
A CHALLENGE

A relatively strong economy through the 80s and early 90s, Thailand struggles with financial institutions and currency fluctuation as do many countries throughout Asia. An effort to stabilize currency and strengthen commerce offers a good outlook for prospects for growth and prosperity into the next decade. Tourism and services have increased and technology, media and telecommunications are making their way into the economic equation. Value for visitors is generally very favorable.

AIRPORT FACILITIES
Airport Code: BKK
City Code: BKK
GREAT

Other Airports:
Chiang Mai
Chiang Rai
Phuket

☛ URBAN CTR
15 miles
45-90 minutes
$10-40 USD

☛ ✈ ALLOW
2 hrs. check-in
2 hrs. transport

Bangkok International Airport has modern terminals with many amenities for first-time arrivals to the city. Two international and one domestic terminal are close to each other. TAT-the Tourism Association of Thailand office at the airport provides great information and services. Select taxis and transport through proper providers. Be careful of free offers. **www.airportthai.or.th** *for a WEALTH of information.*

BE POLITE: *Listen and observe.*

HAVE MANNERS: *Dress and behave as others around you.*

SHOW INTEREST: *Leave your ego behind, ask questions diplomatically.*

MAKE AN EFFORT: *Fit in. Interact. Engage.*

BE POLITE

Observe common greeting practice which includes a slight bow with hands joined flatly together (as in a prayer ritual) with polite greeting. This greeting is acceptable and appreciated in just about any setting. Handshakes are often used in business.

HAVE MANNERS

Punctuality is considered a polite, respectful courtesy. Don't ask demanding "yes" or "no" questions, it's not polite. Adjust your interest and question patterns to include less judgment. Qualify questions so they are not so personally direct. The Thais have many gestures and practices that should be picked up as soon as possible. It's to your advantage to know the conventions of addressing people. Ask someone you trust to quickly explain this to you.

SHOW INTEREST

Use first names if invited to do so or if introduced with such. Note that time and patience are virtues in business and negotiations. Aggressive conversation stating lots of facts is not impressive. Contribute to a conversation with interest in the subject and observations. Topics of interest include unique qualities of Thai life, lifestyles, independence and economic stability. Recognition of Thai commercial influence worldwide fosters a community feeling.

MAKE AN EFFORT

The Thai are impressed if you learn even a few words in their language. Respect and observe local customs especially when they concern the Thai royal family and places of worship. Behave modestly and respectfully to the local culture. Be open to learn about the food and culture that you came to enjoy and experience.

10 Highly Effective Words to "Get By"

1. A Greeting	saah-WAAHt-lee-ee	sawatdee
2. Please	kah-ROO-nAAH	karuna
3. Thank You	kohb-KOON	kob-khon
4. Yes	CHAH-ee	chai
5. No	mae-CHAH-ee, mai aw	mai-chai, mai oua
6. Toilet	hong-NAAH-am	hong naam
7. How Much	nee-rah-KAH-tao-rae	nee-rah-KAH-tao-rae
8. Help	CHOO-ah-ee	chuay
9. Excuse Me	koh-TOOH-s	kor-tose
10. Police	taam-bROO-ah-t	tam-ruat

Great Connections & Community

Jot down important phone numbers, contacts, addresses. Great shops and restaurants---get their Email and Web Address.
SCRIBBLE NOTES and info before, during and after!

Airport & Airline Update

Bangkok Int'l Airport   **www.airportthai.or.th**
A comprehensive and information-rich site. The airport authority of Thailand oversees management of a network of major airports in Thailand. Refer to press releases section for current and ongoing development plans and announcements.

Thai Airways   **www.thaiair.com**
A feature-rich site offering online booking, comprehensive airline services and contacts and current press release announcements addressing interruptions in service and airline issues.

Tourism Authority of Thailand   **www.tourismthailand.org**
An official tourism site with full features and a breadth of information, product and trade news. Only tourism updates.

Moving Forward Advisory: The airport authority's cautious approach to deal with flight and routing changes and anticipated reduced flight schedules to many countries is also the best approach for travellers. Contact your airline directly to get operations schedules. Budget 1 hour more for check-in.

TEAR OUT & TAKE

125

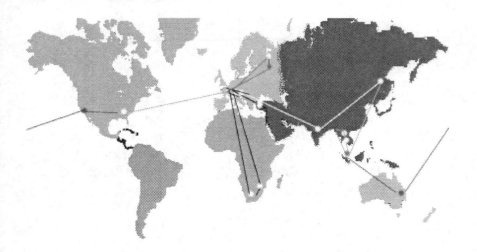

> *GREAT*
> *GOOD*
> *A CHALLENGE*
> *DODGY*
> *CAUTION*

Personal Space
GOOD

Toilets
GOOD

Cleanliness & Bugs
A CHALLENGE

PUBLIC SPACE & PERSPIRATION

A people-dense city with new urban dwellings mixed with old crowded ones keeps people in action and perspiring across all economic levels. Adapt to a more casual style and learn that perspiring is natural. Tropical climates and dense, big cities have a way of testing your preferred and practiced style of hygiene.

TOILETS & TRIBULATIONS

Public facilities in modern structures and in tourist areas cater to Western standards. Many "shabby" and some "budget" appearing type restaurants, entertainment venues and accommodations probably have "shabby" toilets you don't want to spend any time in. Trains offered both Western and Asian-style toilets. Wash sinks and showers are generally separate or unique tiny inventive combination setups. A good toilet isn't that hard to find.

HYGIENE & HIGH JINKS

The lifestyle is big city and traditional. A more relaxed lifestyle in a tropical climate makes it appear that standards are very different. They are relative to their social and economic environment. Tolerance to diverse standards in hygiene is learned through experience. Make the best of it. Drinking and washing face with bottled water offers the best approach.

BUGS:

Geckos rule! Bugs seldom get the best of you because the geckos troll the territory... in many accommodations. Hygiene varies so be cautious of where and what you eat. Get comfortable with screenless open windows and cracked open doors.

Western Style

Asian Style

and everything
i n b e t w e e n

Toilet Stories...

KO SAMUI

Tropical climates offer all kinds of toilet-going trepidations.

In a quaint midrange resort hotel on Bo Phut Beach, Ko Samui, a resort island on the Gulf of Siam side, I was treated to a small fridge and a spacious "bathroom" of the style I was accustomed to. Yippee! A toilet, bathtub, sink and mirror all in one spacious room! I placed a can of Coke in the fridge to chill. I soon fell asleep but only after discovering the glow-in-the-dark geckos crawling on the wall, harmless...and they disappear with light. Not so comforting, but tolerable since they did dissipate my phobia of bumping into bugs in the middle of the night on my way to the bathroom. BUT, the gall of these geckos had me quickly trained. I turned the light on to go to the toilet, I treated myself to a nighttime sip of a cool can of Coke. I took a sip and set it on the night table. Upon my speedy and uneventful return from the toilet I jumped into bed. As my eyes followed my hand as I turned off the light---I jumped at the sight of a gecko taking a sip of my Coke. It startled both of us. And only inches from my pillow, it scurried away. A bit unsettling, THE GALL!!!

The END
of this trip!

Stay tuned for more of the **DARE to** series

Updates and personal pocket guides coming soon.
Check www.InterActiveTraveller.com

Resources

The resources available online and offline have been a tremendous support. While most of my resources were my own journals and collected collateral, I searched hundreds of Web sites and books to verify facts. I did not have a 'grand' source to supply current and consistent information across countries. Just about anything in book form was dated. My main resources were people; I contacted many through email to confirm a fact or situation, and they often referred me to other contacts who shared their knowledge.

In an effort to acknowledge many of my resources I have compiled this short list. There is a wealth of information in book form and online. Thank you for sharing your knowledge online and engaging in conversation with a stranger.

Online:

Maps courtesy of www.theodora.com/maps, used with permission

Russian National Group - Dmitri Nokhov

airports.co.za - Airport of South Africa
airzimbabwe.com
aeroflot.com
singapore-usa.com
switzerlandtourism.ch
travlang.com - Language and Travel Resource
abcnews.com - Country Profiles

travel.state.gov
state.gov

americanexpress.com - Going Global Reports
weissman.com - Weissman Travel Reports
weatherhub.com - Weatherhub Reports
countrywatch.com - Country Reviews
concierge.com - Conde Nast Traveller
travelocity.com - Travelocity, Destination Guides
odci.gov - CIA World Fact Book
worldbiz.com - Worldwide Business Briefings
thejumpseat.com - Airline Employees site
findarticles.com - resource site
airports.org - Airports Council International
worldtravelguide.net - Columbus Publishing

cambodia-web.net - Indochina Project Operations, Ltd.
canbypublications.com - Canby Publications
embassy.org - Embassy contact list
cambodia.org - Cambodia information
asia.com - Asia resource site
businessculture.com - Business Culture Reports
cloanto.com - Cloanto Currency Server
Note: many sites and Web addresses may have changed.

Offline:

Atlanta Journal-Constitution, Travel Section - March 5, 2000

Books:
Cybercafes - A Worldwide Guide for Travelers, *cyberkath@*traveltales.com
Pocket FACT FILE of the World - Longmeadow Press
A Simple Guide to Thailand Customs & Etiquette - Global Books
DOs and TABOOs Around the World - *Roger E. Axtel*
Gestures - The DOs and TABOOs of Body Language Around the World - *Roger E. Axtel*
Dun & Bradstreet's Guide to Doing Business Around the World - *Morrison, Conaway, Douress* - Prentice Hall
Kiss, Bow, or Shake Hands - *Morrison, Conaway, Borden* - Bob Adams, Inc.
Passport India - World Trade Press
Rand McNally - Answer Atlas - Rand McNally

Lonely Planet Guide Books used on trip:
Cambodia
Australia
Russia
South Africa
India
Thailand

About the Author

Jessica Stockwell is a globetrotter who parlayed a French major into a lifelong wanderlust. After working her way through college in the United States and France, she moved into the tourism industry. She served as tourism liaison with the Canadian Consulate General, Tourism Canada in the 1980s and spent 10 years with Swissair. As a market communications executive at Swissair, she initiated research and analysis of trends in travel, travel behavior and travel technology. She led the development of the airline's first Web site and global communications initiative. With an airline industry insider's experience, she knows how it all works and how to work it to your best advantage.

Today, as an Internet media and communications consultant, she advises on Internet strategy, design, function and interface; writes on technology for business travellers; conducts seminars on travel and technology; and speaks on travel trends, personal computing and technology. She also turns as many opportunities as possible into occasions to travel.

DARE to Travel the World–*A Mini Manifesto for Globetrotters* is distilled from the journal Stockwell kept on a six-month, around-the-world trip she took when she left her job at Swissair, unplugged everything and took off. Now she is a champion for international travel, experiential learning and developing life skills.

*Stockwell has pledged a portion of the proceeds from this book to the **Global Fund for Women** (**globalfundforwomen.org**) in recognition of women of courage and inspiration for building community locally, nationally and globally.*